SAN DIEGO'S
TOP BREWERS

Published by Chefs Press, Inc., San Diego, California
www.chefspress.com

Publisher: Amy Stirnkorb
President & CEO: Bruce Glassman
Executive Vice President: Michael D. Pawlenty
Photographs: ©Paul Body, Paul Body Photography, www.paulbodyphoto.com; and Michael D. Pawlenty
Proofreader: Bob Anderson

IMPORTANT PUBLISHER'S NOTE
Every attempt was made to include San Diego's top breweries and craft beer businesses in this project. For those who are not, we have done our best to include them in the back of this book. Their absence from the main body of the book in no way indicates that they are any less important, relevant, or successful than those who are included here.

SPECIAL THANKS
We would like to thank the following people for their generous help in the preparation of this book:
Ryan Ross, of Karl Strauss Brewing Company, for his support and valuable guidance in planning and putting together this book; **Jena Francis**, of Karl Strauss Brewing Company, for supporting the project from the very beginning; **Melody Daversa**, of Karl Strauss Brewing Company, for helping us round up information; **Shawn DeWitt**, of Coronado Brewing Company, and **Adam Carbonell**, of the San Diego Brewers Guild, for helping us to communicate with Guild members; **Jim Crute**, of Lightning Brewery, for his expert review of the "Beer at a Glance" information; **Sage Osterfeld**, of Port Brewing / The Lost Abbey, for his invaluable help in coordinating the logistics of interviews and photo shoots; **Ingrid Croce**, for her gracious help in spreading the word; **Chris Cochran,** of Stone Brewing Co., for his valuable help in coordinating our information gathering; **Randy Clemens** and **Sue Daughters**, of Stone Brewing Co., for their valuable input and coordination assistance; **Mike Mellow**, of Mission Brewery for his help in coordinating the collection of material.

ISBN-13: 978-0-9816222-3-1
ISBN-10: 0-9816222-3-2

First Edition
Printed in China

SAN DIEGO'S
TOP BREWERS
Inside America's Craft Beer Capital

TEXT BY BRUCE GLASSMAN

PHOTOGRAPHY BY PAUL BODY AND MICHAEL PAWLENTY

Chefs Press, Inc.

San Diego, California

INSIDE

FOREWORD

RYAN ROSS, COMMUNITY MANAGER, KARL STRAUSS BREWING COMPANY

San Diego is regarded by many as a perfect vacation destination — if you're lucky, you even call it home. The nickname "America's Finest City" conjures images of beautiful beaches and perfect year-round weather — a place where you can surf in the morning and hit the slopes in the afternoon. But San Diego is about much more than sun and surf. Over the past century, industry in San Diego has undergone immense change. The city has evolved from a commercial fishing hub and military town to a growing center for technology and innovation. This evolution has spawned a burgeoning new industry — an industry that has won the hearts of San Diegans and captivated connoisseurs and gastronomes worldwide. It's San Diego's craft brewing industry.

The humble beginnings of this industry go back to the days when craft beer was simply known as "beer." The so-called Noble Experiment of the 1920s and '30s (aka Prohibition) all but destroyed San Diego's brewing culture and the scores of breweries and taverns that kept our townspeople in suds. Following the repeal of the Volstead Act in 1933, only three San Diego breweries remained; sadly, success for these brewers was short-lived. By the early 1950s, locally brewed beer ceased to exist, while homebrewing remained illegal under federal law.

The next 30 years saw a massive consolidation of the American brewing industry, with a vast majority of American beer sales controlled by three multinational brands. Imports accounted for a small but significant minority. This consolidation limited domestic beer selections and damaged the perception of American-made beer both domestically and abroad. During this "dark age" of American beer, adventurous beer drinkers turned to imports, most settled for the status quo, and a few hoped for a brighter future.

The 1980s brought hope to San Diego's dormant beer culture. Congress repealed legislation that prohibited homebrewing for personal consumption, which led to a rebirth of beer-curious amateurs, hailing from all walks of life and unified by their desire to explore unusual beer styles and to create new recipes to share with friends. San Diego's homebrewing scene spawned clubs and contests where aspiring brewers could share their methods and creations and vie for bragging rights in friendly competitions. Many of these early homebrewers became today's local brewmasters, and their sense of camaraderie and friendly competition has endured to this day.

Homebrewing got another boost in 1982 when California Assemblyman Tom Bates introduced legislation that legalized what would later become known as the "brewpub." By the early 1990s, San Diego's beer culture was back — with brewpubs quenching thirsts and homebrewing-supply shops fueling creativity. Bar owners and restaurateurs soon embraced this emerging culture and helped fuel the demand for "microbrewed" beer. As a result, some brewpubs began bottling and distributing their beers, while other distribution breweries were opening across the county. Many of these breweries were founded by avid homebrewers and former employees of existing breweries. By 1996, the San Diego Festival of Beer was showcasing an impressive range of traditional and experimental local brews — but that was only a prelude of things to come.

By 2000, San Diego's brewers were gaining national recognition for their pioneering methods and innovative offerings. As this passionate and vocal group of brewers burst onto the scene, new vernacular filtered through the beer community. Beers began to be described in terms of their "flavor profiles" — they exhibited hop bitterness, malt character, and yeast-derived esters and phenols. Vocabularies and methods long reserved for wine tasting became commonplace for evaluating and describing beer. Local restaurants and bars started educating staff about different beer styles, and chefs began cooking and pairing their food with beer. *Microbrew* became the terminology of yesteryear and *craft beer* took its place.

Today, San Diego is a cornerstone of brewing innovation and a trendsetter for craft beer culture. The county's brewers are the thought leaders of the industry, the chefs are pioneers in pairing beers with food, the bar and pub owners are tireless advocates of local quality, and the citizens enthusiastically embrace great beer. Over the past decade, San Diego's diverse society of beer evangelists have worked side by side, through good times and bad, to create a welcoming community where beer can once again be enjoyed for all it was meant to be. Visitors often muse about why San Diego is known as America's Finest City; some say it's the weather, others say it's the people, and now some say it's the beer. We say pull up a barstool and enjoy a few local beers with some new friends; you'll soon realize San Diego's a combination of all three. Cheers!

INTRODUCTION

MARTY MENDIOLA, SAN DIEGO BREWERS GUILD

San Diego is a town that's all about beer — really, really good beer! In fact, San Diego is home to more craft breweries than any other county in California, and it's the nation's most award-winning county for craft brewing. The last few years have been especially incredible. At the 2010 World Beer Cup, sponsored by the Brewers Association, San Diego brewers collectively won more awards than any other geographical group in the competition (unless you count the entire United States as a group). San Diego brewers brought home a total of 21 medals from 90 beer style categories, which was more than Germany, Belgium, the United Kingdom, or any of the other 43 *countries* that competed. In addition, San Diego–based Ballast Point Brewing Company claimed one of the three biggest prizes of all: the World Cup Champion Brewery Award in the small brewing company category.

The brewers of San Diego not only brought great honor to their county, they also made their state proud. All in all, California claimed 45 medals total, including the Championship Brewery Awards for both the small and mid-size brewery categories. That meant California breweries won more medals than did Germany, Belgium, and the U.K. combined. (California also took home more medals than Illinois, Colorado, and Oregon combined.) So, clearly California brewers have become the beer world's force to be reckoned with. And San Diego's brewers have claimed their rightful place at the forefront of California's exciting beer scene.

The 2010 Great American Beer Festival was a similar story. San Diego brewers claimed 17 medals, in addition to Pizza Port Brewing Company claiming the honors for both Large Brewpub of the Year (Carlsbad) and Small Brewpub of the Year (San Clemente). This was the fifth time in seven years that San Diego took home a best brewery honor!

To people outside the professional brewing community, it may have seemed as if San Diego brewers came "out of nowhere." Of course, that's far from true. The brewers that brought home medals in 2010 had been brewing, innovating, and perfecting their craft for many years before that.

Most people trace the strong tradition of craft beermaking in San Diego back about 22 years, when

Karl Strauss Brewing Company first opened its doors. Back then, they were the only microbrewery in San Diego, and the first the city had seen in more than 50 years. San Diegans immediately embraced the idea of handcrafted, locally brewed beers, and their enthusiasm inspired a whole host of other young brewers. Within five or six years, an impressive variety of small breweries had opened their doors, including Pizza Port,

Marty Mendiola (left), current SDBG president; Colby Chandler (center) and Adam Carbonell, past SDBG presidents

and then Stone and AleSmith, Ballast Point, and Coronado. By early in the new millennium, Rock Bottom, Green Flash, Lost Abbey, Mission, and Lightning had joined the scene and were followed soon after by some of the youngest guns, including Hess, Iron Fist, Manzanita, Mother Earth, and New English.

The depth and breadth of beer styles being produced in San Diego today is truly staggering. Innovation, creativity, and boundary pushing have become hallmarks for San Diego brewers as a group. Clearly, no one is content to rest on his or her laurels. And all the international recognition has only served to push San Diego's brewers to do more, to become better. Quite often, it's the brewers themselves that push each other. Many brewers attribute the dynamism and productivity of the San Diego brewing scene to the fact that there is a tangible feeling within the community of "friendly competition," where brewers help each other, inspire each other, and root for each other's success. You'd be hard pressed to find a more committed, passionate, and creative bunch of brewing professionals anywhere.

San Diego is now known as "America's Craft Beer Capital" and also as the "Napa Valley of Beer." San Diego Beer Week, which only began in 2009, has already grown to more than 400 events — it's a major happening that draws fans from all over the world.

The brewers and breweries in *San Diego's Top Brewers* represent most of San Diego's larger-scale commercial brewers, but there are many other great breweries and brewpubs that could not be included, and hundreds of small-scale emerging breweries and homebrewers that are also making great beer and keeping the brewing scene vibrant. Of course, this book can inform you and inspire you, but the only way you will truly appreciate the greatness of what's going on in San Diego is to come and taste it all for yourself. We look forward to welcoming you!

BEER AT A GLANCE

BEER TERMINOLOGY: HOW TO READ A CHALKBOARD

Hops

ABV%: Alcohol by volume

OG: Original gravity: the amount of sugar in the wort before fermentation

FG: Final gravity: the amount of sugar in the beer after fermentation

SG: Specific gravity; the amount of sugar in a liquid concentration

IBUs: International Bittering Units: How much hops was used

"NITRO": Actually a mix of nitrogen and carbon dioxide. Many breweries, tasting rooms, and craft beer bars will offer one or two selections "on nitro." The addition of nitrogen gas creates a creamier, richer mouthfeel in a beer.

CONDITIONING: Allowing a beer to condition with yeast present after primary fermentation. This takes place in cask, keg, or bottle.

FIRKIN: A beer container equal to 9 Imperial gallons or 10.8 U.S. gallons

CASK: Historically, a wooden vessel used for conditioning and/or aging beer

BEER ENGINE: A device for manually dispensing beer, usually from a cask

GROWLER: Fresh-fill container used for filling directly from a tap. In the United States a growler is typically a half-gallon jug.

BEER STYLES WITH FOOD PAIRING NOTES

To simplify the dizzying array of available beer styles, its best to categorize them into the two major groups: Ales and Lagers. There are many distinguishing differences between these two major beer categories, but the essential difference lies in yeast and fermentation. In a nutshell, ale yeasts ferment at warmer temperatures and produce fruity and spicy flavors, while lager yeasts ferment at cooler temperatures and yield crisper, cleaner-finishing beers. Here is a quick reference chart that describes the basic categories of beer styles, in order from lightest body to heaviest body. Note that body is not related to alcohol content.

BEER STYLE	ABV	SG	IBU	DESCR
WAHOO WHEAT	4.0%	1.041		
YELLOWTAIL PALE ALE	5.2%	1.010 / 1.050	12	
CALICO AMBER ALE	5.5%	1.009 / 1.051	23	
BIGEYE INDIA PALE ALE	7.0%	1.011 / 1.070	35	
BLACK MARLIN PORTER	6.0%	1.060 / 1.014	91 / 42	
↓ SPECIAL / LIMITED RELEASES ↓	PINT GLASS $2⁹⁹ +TAX			GROWLER JUGS
SCULPIN I.P.A.	7.0%	1.063 / 1.008	7	
Sextant Oatmeal Stout	5.0%	1.052 / 1.014		

WORLD BEER CUP GOLD MEDAL 2010

LAGERS

	FLAVOR PROFILE	TYPICAL ABV%
• PILSNER, HELLES, DORTMUNDER	Crisp & Dry	4% to 6%

These crisp golden lagers will vary in hop character but will be similar in body and lighter malt flavors. They're great additions to richer fare, as their dry effervescence will refresh the palate.

• OKTOBERFEST/MARZEN, MAIBOCK, AMBER LAGER	Smooth & Malty	5% to 7%

These malt forward lagers provide a wealth of caramel, toasted, and nutty malt flavors. They're ideal with the caramelized flavors of grilled meats or toasted flavors of fresh breads and pizzas.

• SCHWARZBIER & BLACK LAGER	Dark & Roasted	5% to 6%

Generous additions of darks malts give these medium-bodied beers roasted, chocolate, and coffee-like malt flavors. They're great additions to BBQ and can even hold their own at the dessert table.

• BOCKBIER & DOPPLEBOCK	Full-Bodied & Robust	6% to 10%

These strong lagers range in alcohol content and have rich caramel and toasted malt flavors. Hop bitterness takes a backseat to forward malt flavors. These beers pair well with roasted meats and tangier cheeses.

ALES

	FLAVOR PROFILE	TYPICAL ABV%
• **AMERICAN PALE, BELGIAN PALE, ENGLISH IPA**	Fruity & Hoppy	5% to 8%

The balance of malts and hops make these styles versatile when pairing with food. They're hoppy enough to temper spice and possess an array of fruity and malty characteristics that complement many foods.

	FLAVOR PROFILE	TYPICAL ABV%
• **WITBIER, HEFEWEIZEN, DUNKELWEIZEN, SAISON, DUBBEL, TRIPPEL**	Fruity & Spicy	4% to 9.5%

Warm fermentations give these beers prominent fruit flavors and varying degrees of spice. They complement dishes that incorporate fresh fruit and their effervescence and common citrus notes makes them great palate cleansers.

	FLAVOR PROFILE	TYPICAL ABV%
• **AMBER, BROWN & RED ALE, ESB, SCOTTISH ALE**	Malty & Mild	5% to 7%

These malt-centric styles provide ample caramel and toasted flavors to pair with. Hop character tends to be mild and won't overpower delicately spiced foods.

	FLAVOR PROFILE	TYPICAL ABV%
• **AMERICAN IPA, AMERICAN IIPA, BLACK IPA**	Very Hoppy	5% to 10%

The intense hop bitterness of these styles makes them ideal for tempering assertively spiced dishes. The prominent citrus character of American hops makes these beers excellent additions to Mexican and Thai-inspired dishes.

	FLAVOR PROFILE	TYPICAL ABV%
• **STOUT & PORTER**	Dark & Roasted	6% to 8+%

These are traditionally brewed with darker malts that lend rich chocolate, roasted, and coffee-like flavors to the beer. Hop character and fruitiness can range from mild to prominent. They're great with roasted meats and chocolate desserts.

	FLAVOR PROFILE	TYPICAL ABV%
• **OLD ALE, BARLEYWINE, WEE HEAVY, BELGIAN GOLDEN & DARK**	Full-Bodied & Robust	7% to 11+%

These rich ales possess varying degrees of hop bitterness but are consistent in their strong fruity and malty character. They're terrific aperitifs or after-dinner additions.

OTHER VARIETIES

	FLAVOR PROFILE	TYPICAL ABV%

- **LAMBIC, GUEUZE** — Fruity & Sour — 5% to 8%

  A typically Belgian style beer that is spontaneously fermented with wild yeasts that enter the wort from the surrounding environment. Brewers will commonly add fruit to a lambic, such as raspberry, peach, or currants.

- **ALTBIER & KÖLSCH BIER** — Crisp, Hoppy, Fruity — 4% to 6%

  The name Altbier means "old beer" in German. The name refers to the brewing method of using an ale yeast — basically brewing it using the lager process, meaning cooler fermentation temperatures. Traditionally, the Alt brewers would store, or lager, the beer after fermentation, leading to a cleaner, crisper beer than is the norm for some top-fermented beers such as British Pale Ale.

THE BREWING PROCESS: FROM BREWHOUSE TO BOTTLING

1. Milled malt goes into the mash tun with hot water, where it sits for 1 to 2 hours. The liquid is strained (lautered) and when this process is complete, the liquid is called "sweet wort."

2. Spent grain is removed, and the wort is transferred to a kettle, where it is brought to a boil.

3. During various stages of the boil, hops are added. Early hop additions impart characteristic bitterness. Late hop additions impart flavor and aroma.

4. When the boil is complete, the wort is cooled down as it is removed from the kettle and transferred to a fermenting vessel, where yeast is added. More hops may also be added toward the end of fermentation — this is known as "dry hopping."

5. After fermentation, the beer is transferred to a storage or "bright" tank, where it sits before kegging and bottling.

ALESMITH BREWING COMPANY

ALESMITH
BREWING COMPANY

{TAP FACTS}

- Began pouring:
  1995

- Brewery size:
  10,700 square feet

- Production per year:
  5,000 barrels

- Recent awards:
  Wee Heavy (gold
  WBC); Decadence
  (bronze WBC); Small
  Brewer/Small Brewery
  of the Year (GABF
  2008)

People always ask AleSmith owner Peter Zien why San Diego has become such a great place for craft beer. Peter's answer is that it's because San Diego's top brewers have traditionally maintained a very close relationship with the homebrewing community. In fact, Peter, who is a past president of the Quality Ale and Fermentation Fraternity (QUAFF), also says that strong homebrewing roots are at the very core of AleSmith's success. "The grassroots beer community is huge here," Peter explains. "And the homebrewers are our biggest supporters. Brewers are smart to take the homebrewers into their community and treat them well." Peter adds that it's often the homebrewers that provide a constant source of critical opinion and an unending enthusiasm for pushing the envelope, trying new things, and improving every aspect of the beer being produced. "It's always been a very nice overlap between the amateurs and the pros here," he notes. "We're all helping each other." Given Peter's perspective, it's not surprising that everyone on the AleSmith brewing team came directly out of the homebrewing community.

The young Peter Zien did not start out with a dream of becoming a brewer. Even though, as early as the 1970s, he constantly found himself yearning for the "better beer out there," it wasn't until the early 1990s that he began to homebrew seriously. It was only after he'd graduated from law school and tried his hand at a home repair finance company in 1991 that he started to develop his brewing skills with a passion. "I'm a hobbyist by nature," Peter admits. "I just like making

The AleSmith Brewing team (left to right):
Ryan Crisp, Tod Fitzsimmons, Peter Zien,
Nick Betteker, Anthony Chen, Bill Batten.

Peter Zien on Beer Education: "We're trying to show people that beer is not just that dumbed-down beverage in cans with the plastic rings on them. It can be quite an exciting beverage, with all the complexity of wine. And our fans know that. And most San Diego beer drinkers now know that beer can be as complex as anything."

a lot of things. I bake. I roast coffee. I make cheeses. I brew beer. I make mustards. Anything I can get my hands on."

As Peter became more involved in the San Diego homebrewing world, he met more people who shared his interests. It was through the homebrewing clubs that Peter met Tod Fitzsimmons, who was part of the original AleSmith team. Peter had been a "big fan of AleSmith for years," and — when he decided to buy the company — Tod became Peter's right-hand man. Peter calls Tod "the heart and soul of AleSmith."

To this day, the "can-do" homebrewing team spirit is evident everywhere in the brewery. Many operations are still done by hand — and often one bottle at a time. For certain products, the entire brewing team will stand together around a bottler and work in unison to fill, cap, foil, and box. Even Peter jumps in and does what's necessary to get the job done.

Abby Heilbron runs AleSmith's tasting room.

AleSmith focuses primarily on beer styles from Belgium, England, and the United States. "One of our great strengths is how we can shift effortlessly between styles," Peter explains. "We can offer you everything from an Extra Pale Ale all the way to our 12% [alcohol content] ABV Speedway Stout with coffee — and nine beers in between. And no two beers are too similar. I think that's really our strength." He's also proud to say that AleSmith makes a beer for just about any kind of drinker — from the crisp, light "X" (the "transition beer" that introduces a novice to the world of quality handcrafted flavors) to the medium-bodied nut browns and maltier beers, to heavily hopped brews, and on to rich, higher-alcohol offerings.

Peter admits that AleSmith can also be seen as a somewhat "eclectic lineup," but he feels that even that is a strength. "I'm very proud of some of our lesser-known beers — like the Wee Heavy Scotch

Special operations, such as bottling the 750 ml bottles, are still done by hand at AleSmith.

Ale — that don't get too much attention but are truly great. That beer is kind of our 'silent warrior' — it's constantly coming back from competitions with awards." Part of Peter's vision for the company is that it offers not only eclectic and interesting styles but also the highest quality possible. "I really want our beers to represent the Rolls Royce segment," he says.

One of Peter's near-term goals is to have AleSmith cheeses available to his followers and fans. "It started with the fact that, as a brewer, I had a lot of spent grain on my hands," Peter explains.

"And that would go to local farmers, who would feed it to their goats, and I would get the milk back. That's where the cheese making began. It scratches the same itch as homebrewing did for me. It's a wonderful world of enzymes and bacteria doing all this work for you — just like with beer."

As soon as he is licensed, Peter says he'll start offering his cheeses to the general public. "I'll not only design cheeses that are meant to go with my beer, I'll also do some that will actually be created with the beer, like my Horny Devil Tome wheel, that has coriander all over the outside of it."

BREWER'S NOTES

ANVIL ESB: Malty, slightly hoppy aroma. Caramel and malty flavors with a perfect balance of imported English hops.

GRAND CRU: Belgian-style. Balance of hoppiness. Complex flavors shift from sweet to tangy to hoppy. Medium-dry finish.

HORNY DEVIL: An authentic Belgian-style ale. Intriguingly complex. Added twist from coriander seeds that impart a refreshing citrus flavor.

IPA: Starts off with pleasantly strong hop flavors, balanced by a firm malt backdrop, then fades to a dry finish with a lingering hoppiness. Medium full-bodied.

LI'L DEVIL: Clean malt flavors with a hint of tangy hop tones. Belgian candi sugar, coriander, and orange peel add a twist. Refreshing, thirst-quenching, and easy to drink.

NAUTICAL NUT BROWN: Rich chocolate malt flavors create complexity and drinkability in this classic English-style Nut Brown Ale. Easy drinking, relatively low-alcohol beer.

OLD NUMBSKULL: West Coast–style barleywine. A huge malt profile and very aggressive dose of premium domestic hops give this a tantalizing complexity, from the aroma to the aftertaste.

SPEEDWAY STOUT: Starts with strong coffee and dark chocolate sensation, then fades to a multitude of toasty, roasty, and caramel malt flavors. Tinge of hops provides the perfect balance to the maltiness.

WEE HEAVY: A classic Scotch Ale. Sweet and malty, with a very subdued dose of hops — just enough to provide balance. Faint touch of smokiness. Full-bodied, smooth, and warming.

X: Refreshing Extra Pale Ale. Light-bodied, smooth on the palate, with a dry finish and superb aftertaste.

> FOR MORE BEER INFO, GO TO WWW.ALESMITH.COM

HAVE A BEER WITH THE BREWER:

Sit down with Peter Zien and a few AleSmith beers:

www.sdtopbrewers.com/alesmith

Chef Schuyler Schultz: AleSmith's Top Chef

When Schuyler Schultz tasted his first bottle of AleSmith beer (Old Numbskull Barleywine), he was still the executive chef at Sonoma Cellar Steakhouse in Las Vegas. As he recalls it, "I remember thinking to myself that this beer is like nothing else I've ever tasted. It was beautifully complex, with a wonderful balance between caramel malt, alcohol sweetness, and bitter American hops. I knew I had to meet the people responsible for making that beer." Well, that's exactly what Schuyler did. In fact, after creating a few beer dinners for AleSmith in Las Vegas, Schuyler moved to San Diego and accepted Peter Zien's offer to become AleSmith's official culinary director. Schuyler's thoughts on the recipe that follows: "Rich, flavorful cuts of meat benefit from pairings with malt-driven, high-alcohol beers. The sweet-sour ground cherries play off of the beer's fruity elements while the bitter endive gives a nod to the hops."

GRILLED BAVETTE STEAK   Serves 4

with Ground Cherry Coulis, Endive Salad, and Savory "French Toast"

Perfect Pairing: AleSmith Old Numbskull Barleywine

FOR THE STEAK:
2 tablespoons sweet soy sauce
1 tablespoon dark soy sauce
3 large garlic cloves, minced
1 serrano chile, sliced
2 tablespoons olive, grapeseed, or canola oil
Freshly ground black pepper
Kosher salt to taste
1 to 2 pounds bavette (flap meat or inside skirt steak), use thickest part, trimmed

FOR THE CHERRY COULIS:
1 pint ground cherries (also known as cape gooseberries or goldenberries)
If ground cherries are unavailable, use golden raisins or dried apricots and then just cover the dried fruit in a small bowl with boiling water and let sit for 1 hour to reconstitute.
2 tablespoons of the water used to reconstitute fruit (omit if using fresh)
1 tablespoon olive, grapeseed, or canola oil
1 teaspoon sherry vinegar
1 teaspoon honey
1/2 teaspoon Dijon mustard
1/4 teaspoon paprika
1 garlic clove, sliced
Pinch kosher salt

FOR THE ENDIVE SALAD:
1 head curly endive or baby frisée
1/4 cup Italian flat leaf parsley, destemmed, and/or other assorted fresh herbs
2 scallions, thinly sliced on the bias
1 teaspoon, or more, olive oil
Ground cherry coulis, for dressing

FOR THE "FRENCH TOAST:"
2 eggs
1/2 cup milk
1 small sprig rosemary, destemmed
1 garlic clove, sliced
1/4 teaspoon paprika
1/4 teaspoon freshly ground black pepper
1/2 teaspoon kosher salt
1 tablespoon butter, for frying
1 crusty baguette, sliced into 1-inch-thick rounds

1. Marinate the steak: Mix all the ingredients together (except for the meat) then smear the mixture all over the steak. Refrigerate to marinate for as long as you can, up to 8 hours.
2. Make the coulis: Purée all the ingredients in a blender or food processor until smooth and emulsified. Adjust liquid if necessary.
3. Prepare the salad: Select small, tender, light-colored inner leaves for the salad. Toss greens together with the parsley, scallions, and the ground cherry coulis mixed with additional olive oil.
4. Grill the steak: Over very hot coals, grill until just before medium-rare and a nice crust has developed. Let the meat rest, covered with aluminum foil, for 5 minutes. Slice thinly against the grain of the meat.
5. Make the "French toast": Mix all the ingredients together (except for the bread) until the eggs are thoroughly beaten. Soak the bread slices in the mixture, turning frequently, until they are thoroughly soaked with liquid. Melt the butter in a medium pan over medium-high heat. Fry each bread round until golden brown on each side and the interior of each has set.
6. To serve: Spoon some coulis around a serving plate in a decorative manner. Place two slices of the "French toast" slightly off-center. Place a small amount of salad on the plate. Drape slices of steak over the salad and "French toast." Garnish with fresh herbs.

Chef Schuyler created this great dessert to highlight the amazing qualities of AleSmith's Barrel-Aged Speedway Stout. "This version of a traditional British pub dessert utilizes flavors similar to those found in many 'dessert' beers, such as toffee, caramel, molasses, dates, and dried fruit. Using an intense bourbon-barrel-aged beer as the liquid in the cake infuses it with rich, dark flavors."

ENGLISH TOFFEE PUDDING CAKE Serves 8

Perfect Pairing: AleSmith Speedway Stout

1 cup flour, plus 1 tablespoon
1 teaspoon baking powder
³/₄ cup raisins and/or chopped dates
4 tablespoons unsalted butter, softened, plus 3 tablespoons, for topping
³/₄ cup granulated sugar
1 large egg, lightly beaten
1¹/₄ cups dark, sweet, full-bodied beer
   (preferably bourbon-barrel-aged; chef suggests AleSmith Speedway Stout, Sam Adams Triple Bock, or Goose Island Bourbon County)
1 teaspoon baking soda
1 teaspoon pure vanilla extract
5 tablespoons dark brown sugar, firmly packed
2 tablespoons heavy cream
Pinch kosher salt

1. Preheat the oven to 350ºF.
2. Butter an 8-inch round cake pan.
3. Sift the 1 cup flour and the baking powder together.
4. Toss the raisins and/or chopped dates with the remaining 1 tablespoon of flour. Set aside.
5. In a mixer, beat together the 4 tablespoons of butter and the sugar until light and fluffy. Beat in the egg on low speed and add roughly ¼ of the flour mixture; mix until smooth. Add the remaining flour mixture and mix until just incorporated.
6. In a saucepan, bring the beer to a simmer. In a small bowl, combine the raisins/dates, baking soda, vanilla, and simmering beer. Add this mixture to the batter and beat until well blended. Pour the mixture into the cake pan.
7. Bake for 30 minutes, or until set and well-browned.
8. Remove the cake from the oven and preheat the broiler.
9. In a small saucepan, heat the remaining 3 tablespoons butter, brown sugar, cream, and salt until the mixture simmers. Simmer until thickened and bubbly (about 3 minutes). Pour this topping over the hot cake.
10. Broil the cake until the topping bubbles while watching carefully to prevent burning. Cool the cake briefly.
11. **To serve:** Serve warm with whipped cream, sweetened to taste, with vanilla, and sliced fresh figs.

BALLAST POINT BREWING COMPANY

{TAP FACTS}

- Began pouring:
  HBM 1992; BP 1996

- Brewery size:
  25,000 square feet

- Production:
  24,000 barrels

- Recent awards:
  Fathom IPL (gold
  GABF); Small Brewery
  (WBC champ); Sculpin
  IPA (gold WBC); Piper
  Down Scot Ale (gold
  WBC); Fathom IPL
  (gold WBC)

To look at the brewery from the outside, you'd never know that it houses one of San Diego's most popular and exciting beermaking facilities. But that's Ballast Point all over. The brewery's exterior mirrors the dedicated team inside: humble and unassuming on the outside but bursting with creative energy and talent on the inside.

Tucked inside a typical SoCal office park complex, Ballast Point's production area is chock-full of fermentation tanks, bottling equipment, stills, casks, and bulk ingredients of all possible kinds. It's a beehive of activity, and everyone is immersed in producing one of the brewery's many distinctive and delicious beverages — recipes that at some earlier point were the brainchild of master brewers Yuseff Cherney or Colby Chandler.

Left to right: Colby Chandler, Yuseff Cherney, and Jack White

Like many a top brewer, owner and founder Jack White started his beer journey as a homebrewer. Like many a college student, Jack developed his taste for beer while in school (UCLA). As his palate expanded, he found himself more and more frustrated by a lack of quality

BALLAST POINT
BREWING COMPANY
IMPERIAL STOUT
SEA MONSTER
IMPERIAL PORTER

Amber Crocker rules the Ballast Point tasting room.

choices. That inspired him to start brewing in his own backyard.

It didn't take long for Jack to get really good at homebrewing, and it took even less time for him to realize that there were relatively few places he could go to get quality ingredients or equipment. So, in 1992, Jack decided to "take the leap" and open his own homebrewing supply shop. "I kind of decided at that time that I was young enough to try something like this and make a big mistake and still have time to get into something else," Jack says with a smile. One of the first customers to walk into his Home Brew Mart was a young and very talented homebrewer named Yuseff Cherney. "He came walking into the store, I talked to him a little bit, and I hired him basically the next day," Jack recalls. "He was also Home Brew Mart's first real employee. Before that, it was just me — I was the owner, founder, CEO, the brewer, and stock boy, too."

Jack and Yuseff soon found themselves discussing techniques, collaborating on ideas, and dreaming about bigger things. That's when they decided to move Jack's backyard brewing rig to the Home Brew Mart location and get their California Type 23 license for small beer manufacturers. Soon after, in 1996, Ballast Point Brewing was officially born.

Bottles get a dose
of liquid nitrogen
before filling on the
bottling line.

Home Brew Mart (above and below), where Ballast Point still brews custom beers and sells homebrewing supplies to the public.

From the earliest days, Yuseff and Jack were looking to make great beers across a wide spectrum of styles and flavors. As Yuseff explains it, "I want to make a wide range of beer styles but make each one unique within its category; to do stuff no one else is doing." Their skill and vision paid off. It wasn't long before Home Brew Mart customers were clamoring for more and more of what Ballast Point was making. By 2004, they could no longer keep up with demand. It was unavoidable — they'd have to move into larger quarters and start making a whole lot more beer.

Today, Ballast Point faces a similar problem — albeit a good problem to have. Great press, national and international recognition, and numerous awards and medals (including the 2010 World Beer Cup Champion Brewer in the small brewery category) have meant the brewery is still struggling to keep up with demand. "2010 was definitely the biggest year so far for us," Jack says. "Winning the World Beer Cup, winning four different gold medals for three different beers … all the things that have happened seemed to have culminated in this one year, and now we can't even come close to keeping up." Even at more than 10,000 barrels a year in production, Ballast Point is (temporarily) unable to supply everyone who wants what they make. "We just can't make enough," explains Marketing Manager Earl Kight. "We always joke that we have the best problem a brewery can have."

When you ask other members of the San Diego brewing community to name a brewery that's doing cool stuff, Ballast Point always comes up. That's partly because they're always experimenting and looking to push in new directions. Yuseff and

specialty brewer Colby Chandler are major forces in keeping Ballast Point innovative. At the original Home Brew Mart location, Colby develops new recipes and brews them in small batches. He likes to say that that's where a lot of Ballast Point's new beers are "birthed." "And then, when that beer becomes an ornery teenager, we send it on up to the Scripps Ranch facility."

Colby, who is a past president of the San Diego Brewers Guild, has influenced many young brewers in the area and has a long record of brewing innovations. Of all the beers he's helped to create, he's most proud of the extremely popular Sculpin IPA. "That beer was originally brewed with Home Brew Mart employees. In fact, I took two similar recipes from two different employees (who still work there), I sprinkled in a few of my ideas and knowledge, and that's how Sculpin came around. Considering that it's been rated the number one IPA on BeerAdvocate.com for nearly two years, that's pretty cool."

For Colby, Home Brew Mart remains a constant source of inspiration for new beers. His daily interaction with all kinds of homebrewers provides him with a constant source of feedback, ideas, and

encouragement. As far as new recipes go, Colby likes to play with anything and everything. "I just did a beer where I used all local, indigenous ingredients. I went out and picked manzanita berries and white sage, and used local honey, pine nuts, all that kind of stuff. It's kind of a San Diego Farmhouse Ale," he explains.

Yuseff is also pursuing new directions, even beyond beer. During the past few years, he has begun distilling spirits at the brewery. "A lot of my work recently has gone into developing the recipes and building the brand for these spirits," Yuseff explains. "It's kind of the next step in brewing — you learn how to brew and then the next thing you want to do is turn that beer into whiskey." "The spirits are a natural progression," Jack says, "because distillation comes after the fermentation process." In addition to their Three Sheets Rum, their Old Grove Gin, and their feisty Bloody Mary Mix (one of Yuseff's inspirations), they will be releasing a handcrafted bourbon called Devil's Share. "With that release, Ballast Point will be the only bourbon producer in San Diego, and the first since Prohibition," Yuseff explains. Jack adds, "We're basically trying to have fun, and we're doing the things that we like to do. Trying to keep it creative."

BREWERS' NOTES

BIG EYE IPA: Bitter, hoppy flavor from Centennial hops.

PALE ALE: Subdued fruitiness is a perfect complement to the crispness of the wheat and maltiness of the Munich malt.

SCULPIN IPA: Testament to Home Brew Mart's humble beginnings. Showcases bright, crisp flavors and aromas of apricot, peach, mango, and lemon.

BLACK MARLIN PORTER: Rich, dark, and chocolatey Porter with a distinctive American hop character. Goes great with hearty foods and, surprisingly, with dessert. Blend Black Marlin with Big Eye IPA for a treat called the Black Eye.

CALICO AMBER ALE: Rich complexity comes from four types of malt — but it's those distinct American hops that offer a crisp bitterness and unique floral aroma. Proprietary yeast creates fruity, Madeira-like richness.

WAHOO WHEAT: Belgian Witbier-style. Light and refreshing with citrus character from orange peel and coriander. Hazy appearance comes from the unmalted wheat.

> FOR MORE BEER INFO, GO TO WWW.BALLASTPOINT.COM

Yuseff Cherney (above) and Colby Chandler (below)

HAVE A BEER WITH THE BREWER:

Sit down with Colby Chandler and a few Ballast Point beers:

www.sdtopbrewers.com/ballastpoint

Chef Kyle Bergman: The Grill at The Lodge at Torrey Pines

The Lodge at Torrey Pines is world renowned, not only for the golf course nestled against it, but also for the cuisine offered by its two main restaurants, A.R. Valentien and The Grill. At The Grill, Chef Kyle Bergman has made it his personal mission (along with Grill Manager Stephen Kurpinsky, in photo) to celebrate and highlight great craft beermakers — from San Diego and beyond. On the last Wednesday of every month, Kyle presents his "Craft Food & Beer Series," a special menu that pairs exciting dishes with great beers. The two recipes that follow are favorites from Kyle's Ballast Point menu. "I really liked the Serrano Pale Ale for the trout," Kyle says. "It was clean and crisp, but it also had that really nice pepper flavor to it. It had enough heat that with the raita (Indian-style yogurt-cucumber sauce) and the smoked trout, it would really clean your palate off, refresh it, and make you want to come back for more."

SMOKED RUBY TROUT   Serves 4

with Pink Pepper Raita and English Cucumber Salad

Perfect Pairing: Ballast Point Roasted Serrano Pale Ale (or regular Pale Ale)

FOR THE TROUT:
4 fresh ruby trout fillets
6 cups granulated sugar
2 cups salt
8 tablespoons cracked coriander, toasted
Wood chips for smoking

FOR THE RAITA:
8 cups plain yogurt
3 tablespoons pink peppercorns
2 cloves garlic, minced
1 nub ginger, peeled and minced (about 2 tablespoons)
1 cup English cucumber, peeled, seeded, and finely diced
1 teaspoon cumin seeds, toasted and ground
Fresh lemon juice to taste
Salt and pepper to taste

FOR THE HERB VINAIGRETTE:
1 cup champagne vinegar
2 medium shallots, diced
1 cup fresh herbs (tarragon, chive, basil, sage), chopped
3 cups extra virgin olive oil

FOR THE SALAD AND GARNISH:
1 English cucumber, peeled, washed, and sliced thin
1 bunch watercress, washed and trimmed
4 hard-boiled eggs

1. Prepare the trout: Lay out the trout fillets, skin side down, and sprinkle them liberally with sugar, salt, and coriander. They must be packed down and thickly coated. Allow them to rest for no more than 20 minutes, then rinse them with water. Pat the fillets dry and refrigerate uncovered overnight to dry out.

2. Make the raita: Combine all the ingredients and refrigerate overnight.

3. Soak wood chips in water for 1 to 2 hours and place them in a grill. Cold smoke the trout for 45 minutes. (For cold smoking: heat the grill with just a few briquettes, or on very low heat, just to get the wood chips smoking. Then turn off the heat and add the fish.)

4. Make the vinaigrette: Combine all the ingredients in a blender or whisk together in a bowl, incorporating the oil last in a slow, steady stream.

5. Slice the cucumber and toss in a bowl with the watercress and the vinaigrette.

6. To serve: Spoon 3 to 4 tablespoons of raita on each plate. Carefully remove the skin from the trout, starting at the tail. Place the trout on top of the sauce. Carefully place the salad on top and around the fish and sauce. Cut the eggs in half and place them with the salad.

Chef Kyle loves to pair this recipe with the big, rich, bitter flavors of Ballast Point's Sculpin. He likes the way the beer, the richness of the duck, and the sweetness of the pork belly all play off each other. Kyle also goes out on a limb to say, "Sculpin doesn't actually have any ginger flavor in it, but it has flavors that are evocative of ginger, which I really like with this dish. So that's where I was going with this pairing."

DUO OF BALLAST POINT DUCK BREAST AND PORK BELLY
Serves 2
with Potato Confit and Red Cabbage Braise

Perfect Pairing: Ballast Point Sculpin IPA

FOR THE BRAISED PORK BELLY:
8 cups pork, duck, or chicken stock
2 carrots, thickly sliced
2 yellow or white onions, roughly chopped
3 stalks celery, roughly chopped
1 head garlic, peeled
1 cup honey
1 cup salt
1 bunch fresh thyme
3 bay leaves
1¹/₂ pounds pork belly
4 cups Ballast Point Pale Ale

FOR THE POTATO CONFIT:
1 large Idaho potato, peeled and halved
   lengthwise, with the ends removed to
   form 2 squat half-cylinders
2 tablespoons olive oil
1 pound sweet butter
1 bunch fresh thyme
2 lemons, zested
2 bay leaves

FOR THE CABBAGE:
1 large red cabbage, shredded
2 carrots, peeled and sliced into rounds
2 stalks celery, thickly sliced on a bias
1 medium yellow or white onion, sliced into
   thick wedges
2 cloves garlic, peeled and crushed
2 bay leaves
2 cups Ballast Point Pale Ale
¹/₂ cup snow pea pods, for garnish

FOR THE DUCK:
2 duck breasts, trimmed and scored
Salt and pepper to taste
3 tablespoons whole-grain mustard

1. Make the pork marinade: Mix together all the ingredients (except the pork and the beer) and divide mixture in half. To the first half, add the pork belly and the beer. Cover and refrigerate for 2 days. Reserve second half in refrigerator.

2. Make the pork belly: Preheat oven to 275°F. Remove the pork from the marinade and place it in a medium baking dish. In a

medium pot, bring the second half of the mixture to a boil, add it to the pork, and bake for 2 to 4 hours, or until very tender. Remove from the oven, cover with foil, and set aside.

3. Make the potatoes: Preheat the oven to 300°F. In a medium sauté pan, sear the potatoes in oil until they are brown on both sides. Remove them from the pan. Melt the butter with all the other ingredients, plus a little water. Divide the potatoes into two ramekins, cover with the melted butter mixture, and bake in the oven until a small knife slips in easily, about 1 hour.

4. Make the cabbage: In a large pot, combine the cabbage, carrots, celery, onion, garlic, bay leaves, and the beer (reserve 2 tablespoons for the mustard). Braise the vegetable mixture on low heat until tender. Set aside.

5. Make the duck: Season the duck with salt and pepper. In a hot sauté pan, sear the breasts skin side down, then reduce heat to medium-low and finish cooking to desired temperature (175°F for medium) on the stovetop.

6. To serve: Warm up all of the components. Mix the ale into the mustard. On one side of the plate, spoon half the braised cabbage mixture, then slice the duck breast and lay it on top. On the other side of the plate, place one of the potatoes, alongside a small pool of the mustard. Place the pork on top of the mustard and finish with a little of the hot pork braising liquid. Garnish with raw pea pods.

BLIND LADY ALE HOUSE

FROM THE MOMENT YOU STEP INTO BLIND LADY ALE HOUSE, you know it's more than just a bar — it's a meeting place that's part of a real community. Building a sense of community is at the core of Lee Chase's mission; he's one of the owners along with his wife Jenniffer, Jeff Motch, and Clea Hantman.

Lee and his partners have been members of the Normal Heights community for years. The old historic building on Adams Avenue near 34th Street was always a particular favorite of Lee's. Built in the 1920s, it once housed a company called The Automatic Venetian Blind Lady, which did window coverings, cleaning, and repairs. When he uncovered that little piece of history, Lee recalls, "my first thought was that sounded like the kind of place Tom Waits would go hang out — that sounds good."

The journey to becoming a tavern owner was a bit different for Lee than for most. He is a master brewer who had brewed for four companies (Stone Brewing Co. for nearly 10 years) before starting Blind Lady. Lee explains that he was more inspired to serve beer than to brew it for a bunch of reasons: "Luckily, this space was not only six blocks from my house, it was also in San Diego. With so much good beer already going on here, it wasn't such a necessity to actually make it ourselves. It's no sweat to populate 27 faucets with really good beer, without any hassle."

Aside from providing a venue for drinking great local craft beer, Lee sees his mission at Blind Lady as being a lot about community. The community aspect is also something that Lee feels distinguishes Blind Lady Ale House from other pizza places or beer bars. "We wanted to make a place that has a bigger community feel by the way

Below (left): A pint of Automatic Brewing Ale; (middle): BLAH offers a huge selection of great craft brews; (right): house-smoked pork brat with homemade kimchee.

Above (left): Patrons love BLAH's open, communal feeling; (right): Lee Chase

we designed it. The thought was to keep the menu fairly simple but make it excellent — and the same with the beers. Then give the people the space they need to associate with each other. And that's the community part of it." Lee and his partners spent many hours discussing how the design of the tavern should actually work. "Before we opened, the thought was 'it's a really bad economy, there's not a lot of money, but people still have a taste for good food and a thirst for good beer. So, why don't we give them space, give them a place to meet and discuss things, and — from those discussions — maybe businesses develop.' If we can help nurture that a little bit, then we might also stay in business."

In his unique position, Lee gets a wide perspective on San Diego's "beer culture." He is particularly encouraged to see that craft beer is enjoying an ever broader following, not just among "beer geeks" but also among the general population. "I'm excited to see that within the group of people we see here on a regular basis not all of them are all that 'nerdy' about beer. That means that beer has really broken out of its shell. It's really cool to think that small breweries can sell beer to people who don't necessarily follow the small brewery culture."

BREAKWATER BREWING CO.

{TAP FACTS}

- Began pouring: 2009

- Brewery size: 2,000 square feet

- Production per year: About 650 barrels

- Up to 12 styles produced

- Only San Diego brewer to also produce mead

- Recent awards: Broken Skeg (gold WBC); Del Mar Jetty IPA (gold SDIBF)

Just a few blocks from the beach in Oceanside, Breakwater Brewing Co. embodies the laid-back SoCal spirit of sand, surf, and sun. And their lineup of brews reflects a fun, playful attitude that lets you know they make great beer but they don't take themselves too seriously (they do their tasting flights on little wooden surfboards).

It's not that the guys who run Breakwater don't have the qualifications. Head brewer Lars Gilman learned his craft in some notable places. After homebrewing for many years, Lars explains that he "got carried away enough" by homebrewing that by 2001 he decided to attend the Siebel Institute of Technology and World Brewing Academy in Chicago, where he was living at the time. "I took the course in brewing technology and used that as a way to get a foot in the door at any brewery in the Chicago area." He found a position at Goose Island Brewery, where he worked his way up from scrubbing kegs to running the bottle-filling line. Then he decided he wanted to return to his native Southern California. "I started canvassing breweries all over the state," Lars recalls, "and I found a job as a brewer at Stone [Brewing Co.], where I worked for about two years (2002–2004) before leaving to open HydroBrew, my own homebrewing supply shop."

Little wooden surfboards hold Breakwater's tasting flights.

Visitors can choose from more than 30 taps that showcase local craft beer.

Lee Chase was Stone's head brewer while Lars was there, and Lars considers himself fortunate to have had Lee as a colleague. Lars still refers to Lee as "the most knowledgeable brewer I have ever met. He is also adulated, and with good reason."

The actual preparation of the site for Breakwater began in 2008, but due to a long and arduous inspection and permitting process, the beers weren't actually flowing from the taps until January 2009. The facility houses a bar and restaurant, along with a 7-barrel brewery that produces about 650 barrels per year. Currently, all of Breakwater's beer is distributed at the restaurant — there are growler (half-gallon jug) fills, but no bottles. Lars likes to brew a wide variety of styles and likes using a varied

palette of flavors: "I try to brew a little bit of this and a little bit of that," Lars says. "I don't tend to do a whole lot of lagers, though we have made a pilsner." (He points out that Breakwater's previous brewer, Kirk McHale, produced an awesome Dopplebock that won gold at the 2010 World Beer Cup.) "Even though it's pretty much all ales in the lineup right now, it covers a lot of ground, including IPAs, Belgians, and we even have a mead with raspberries and hibiscus. I'm not completely sure, but I may be the only brewer in San Diego making mead commercially." Lars brews about 12 different styles regularly and would like to expand his sour beer offerings, perhaps even bottling them exclusively. "Sour beers are time consuming and also a labor

Breakwater Brewing Co.
Oceanside CA

of love," he explains, "so that may be a project a little further down the road."

The Breakwater organization is perhaps a bit unique — it's not your usual family-owned operation, nor is it a big corporate-owned endeavor. The company actually belongs to a dozen Breakwater employees — it's a sort of "beer cooperative." On any given day, one or two of the shareholders can be found working the pizza oven or overseeing the food service. Another shareholder may be behind the bar, and still another may be managing the front of the house. All in all, the atmosphere is one of teamwork with a shared dedication to making the space as open and friendly as it can be.

Lars and his partners are truly excited by the growth they have seen — not only in their business but also in the San Diego craft beer business. "I think one of the nice things about the craft brewing industry is that competition is not necessarily a bad thing," Lars says. "I feel very fortunate to be brewing here in San Diego County, because there are so many good breweries that it brings people around to everyone — a lot of people want to visit several breweries in a day — that's good for business. I consider myself fortunate to have landed in the right place at the right time, I guess."

BREWER'S NOTES

BEACH HONEY ALE: Light-bodied, easy drinking ale that's brewed with more than a gallon of local grapefruit honey per barrel.

FULL NELSON PALE ALE: Medium-bodied; brewed with 100% New Zealand–grown Nelson Sauvin hops.

KALI KUSH: A specialty Pale Ale, brewed with a touch of local, wild-grown sagebrush.

HILL STREET HIBISCUS: An ale brewed with a good deal of hibiscus flowers. Tropical, fruity, tart, and whimsical.

RAIL SLIDE RED: A hoppy, West Coast–style red ale.

DMJ IPA: A classic, intensely hoppy West Coast–style IPA.

O'PIRATE STOUT: Smooth and malty oatmeal stout with a mouth-filling, creamy head.

PROCRASTINATION: A barrel-aged lambic-style Belgian sour ale brewed with a touch of locally grown passion fruit; dry, tart, and fruity.

MAVERICK'S DOUBLE IPA: A massive hops monster, brewed with three pounds of hops per barrel.

OLD BLUE EYES: A smooth and malty "Old Ale"–style beer, aged on oak chips.

TRIPPEL THREAT: A strong Belgian-style golden ale with an aromatic yeast profile and a crisp, clean finish.

RASBISCUS MEAD: A dry, sparkling honey wine, flavored with raspberries and hibiscus flowers.

> FOR MORE BEER INFO, GO TO
WWW.BREAKWATERBREWING.COM

HAVE A BEER WITH THE BREWER:

Sit down with Lars Gilman and a few Breakwater beers:

www.sdtopbrewers.com/breakwater

Chef Shannon Sager: Breakwater Brewing Co.

Shannon loves this recipe because it is so easy and so delicious. It's a particular favorite when Breakwater is hosting a large event and tasty food in large quantities is the main goal. You can do this recipe in an oven or on a grill, or you can use both. Shannon also recommends that you slather the finished ribs with your favorite BBQ sauce.

BREAKWATER STOUT RIB TIPS   Serves 4 to 6

Perfect Pairing: Breakwater O'Pirate Stout

4 tablespoons granulated garlic
2 tablespoons freshly ground black pepper
2 tablespoons red pepper flakes
2 tablespoons oregano, dried
2 tablespoons basil, dried
4 tablespoons salt
4 tablespoons olive oil
4 cups O'Pirate Stout
2 large racks baby back pork ribs

1. Make the marinade: In a large mixing bowl, combine all the dry ingredients. Whisk in the oil.
2. Brush the mixture generously onto both sides of the ribs and set them inside a roasting pan. Add the stout, trying to cover as much of the ribs as possible. Marinate in the refrigerator overnight, or for a minimum of 12 hours.
3. Remove the ribs from the marinade.
4. Cook the ribs. For the oven: Preheat to 425°F and cook the ribs for 15 minutes. Turn down the heat to 250°F and cook for 1½ hours (or until the meat falls away from the bone). For the grill: Preheat to 250°F to 300°F (low) and cook for about 2 hours (or until the meat falls away from the bone).
5. Finish with your favorite BBQ sauce (Stone Brewing Co. makes an awesome one!)

CHICKS FOR BEER

INGRID QUA IS ON A MISSION: She wants to build a new legion of women craft-beer drinkers. As the owner of the High Dive Bar & Grill on Morena Boulevard, Ingrid decided to start the Chicks for Beer club in June 2010. She says she wants to "provide a forum for women to learn about and enjoy craft beer."

"Chicks for Beer is a little bit different than most beer clubs," Ingrid explains. "Most of the other forums are not as social — what I wanted to do was to put together a fun social club for women, some of whom may possibly know a lot about beer, but also for those who don't know anything about beer." Ingrid's initial main focus was to highlight San Diego craft breweries. "Each month we have a local brewer come down, bring his specialty beers, and our members get six tastings with food pairings, and a pint. They also get to talk to the brewer, and they get to know that brewery. It's been a huge success." So far, more than 300 women are affiliated with the club.

When she first started out, Ingrid admits that even she knew relatively little about craft beer. She really credits the brewing community of San Diego for helping her to realize her dream. "I am so privileged to live in San Diego," Ingrid says, "not only because we have some of the most amazing craft breweries in the world, but also because the craft community here is so open and willing to help out. When

Below (left): Shrimp ceviche from a Ballast Point menu; (right): Jamming on a Tuesday night.

Above (left): Chicks for Beer meets in the bar's private patio; (right): Ingrid Qua, founder of Chicks for Beer.

I began, I went to Colby at Ballast Point, Shawn at Coronado — even Karl Strauss — and I asked them for help. They actually sat down with me and taught me about beer! Everybody was so open and excited about bringing another craft beer bar into the community."

Ingrid likes the fact that many members have come without any prior beer-drinking experience. "A lot of the women have come on their own," she says, "and I would say about 40 percent of the women come to the group never having had a craft beer." So learning and breaking down misconceptions is a big part of the experience. "A lot of women, they're used to drinking Stella [Artois] — they're used to drinking these lighter beers. They're also afraid of the darker beers, when in reality, most of the darker beers have all of the flavors that women love. The chocolate, the coffee that you get in porters and stouts, for example. Those are the fun ones to introduce to women. They realize, 'Wow! this is a really sweet, fun beer!"

"Before one event," Ingrid recalls, "a lot of the women were saying they hated IPAs. Then we paired lemon bars with Ballast Point's Sculpin IPA, and the women were so surprised that all this citrus came out in the Sculpin, and how it tasted so different." Ingrid loves it when she sees women "switching over" to beers that, previously, they would never have even touched. "That's what makes it fun to me!" she smiles.

CORONADO BREWING COMPANY

{TAP FACTS}

- Began pouring:
  1995

- Brewery size:
  1,000 square feet

- Production per year:
  4,500 barrels

- Bestselling brew:
  Orange Ave. Wit

- Only brewing company
  in Coronado

The Orange Avenue setting is idyllic: in one direction, a few blocks away, is Coronado's world-famous beach; a few blocks the other way is the island's gorgeous marina and ferry landing. Coronado Brewing Company (CBC) is perfectly situated — in more ways than one. Not only is it the only brewing company in Coronado, it is also one of San Diego's fastest-growing breweries, consistently recognized for an outstanding lineup of handcrafted brews.

Brothers Rick (left) and Ron Chapman

Coronado Brewing Company started out as a collaboration between two sets of brothers who all had a desire to create a great brewery and restaurant. Brothers Ron and Rick Chapman partnered with brothers Tim and Shawn DeWitt to found the company in 1995. All four shared a strong entrepreneurial spirit, a love for great food and great beer, and a conviction that Coronado needed a brewery it could truly call its own.

Shawn DeWitt, who trained at La Jolla Brewing Company before CBC officially opened in 1996, became Coronado's brewmaster. "My route to becoming a brewmaster was a little different than most," Shawn says. "I was never a homebrewer — in fact, I never even had any interest in brewing. I was a barista for a café here in Coronado."

accessible "food" beers. "We do make a bunch of bigger beers," Shawn says. "We like to get creative and do stuff like our Black IPA, our Red Devil, and our Bourbon Barrel Imperial Smoked Brown. That's the stuff we really have fun with."

Many of CBC's recipes are developed by the young and talented Sean Farrell. "I like to work with variations of the Belgian-, German-, and English-style beers, mostly the kinds of beers that I want to drink," Sean explains. As head brewer, Sean is constantly developing new recipes and new ideas for beers he hasn't yet done. "The biggest challenge in doing different types of beers is getting the right yeasts," Sean says. "And buying a new yeast can be expensive — like $500. So, to make it cost effective, when we buy a yeast to do a Belgian or a lager, we do a series. That means we can brew a whole bunch of beers from the same yeasts and make enough beer to cover our costs. Every year, we do a Belgian series, a lager series, and an English series — which adds great variety to what we have on tap — and every year I change what those beers are going to be." CBC's 2011 Belgian series included a Belgian Pale, a Belgian Brown, and a Belgian IPA (a hybrid of a Trippel and an American IPA), all using a Trappist yeast strain. Thinking back, Sean admits that his favorite was the Belgian Pale. "The big beers are fun to drink, but I like taking home a growler and having more than one."

After his return from Oktoberfest in Europe in 2010, Sean was particularly inspired by the beers of

From the beginning, Shawn's primary vision for brewing at CBC has been to create what he calls "drinkable beers." As he explains it, "Being that we are a restaurant, we want accessible beers that are great-tasting, not too filling, and go perfectly with food." But the CBC tap lineup is not strictly about

What's Special About the San Diego Brewing Community?
"It's a very synergistic relationship," Ron Chapman says. "Even though we're all competing for the same retail dollars in the market, we always help each other out. It's a very competitive but very cooperative market. It's nice to be a part of that."

Belgium. "They do have a lot of big-flavored beers there," he explains, "but they're all highly drinkable. That's what I'm going for. Something that has a lot of flavor, but something you can also have more than one pint of."

As San Diego has gained notoriety among beer lovers around the world, demand for its craft brews has risen considerably. Coronado Brewing Company, like its fellow breweries, has enjoyed the benefits of a greatly increasing fan base. In 2009, CBC produced a total of 2,500 barrels. By the end of 2010, their production had almost doubled. They produce about 4,500 barrels now and do all their bottling and kegging right there at the restaurant.

"We have grown a lot in the past three years, especially on the distribution side of our business," Ron Chapman explains. "We're available in 10 different states, carried by 17 different distributors, and that's about all we can do right now with the quantity we produce. So we're now in the process of building a production facility. We're identifying the parts of San Diego that we'd like to do that in, and we have a lot of work to do."

In addition to being one of San Diego's top

brewers, Shawn DeWitt has also been the vice president of the San Diego Brewers Guild. His involvement in the group has given him a unique "big picture" perspective on the area's brewing scene. "There so many great brewers here," Shawn says. "The guys at Ballast Point and Green Flash are doing really exciting things. Then there's Stone and Karl Strauss and so many others. I think a lot of it is that we all seem to push each other. We all like getting quite creative, and we're all competitive with each other, but in a really good, friendly way."

BREWERS' NOTES

CORONADO GOLDEN: This ale is smooth, light in flavor, crisp, delicately hopped, and very similar to a European-style pilsner.

ORANGE AVE. WIT: Our spiced California-style Wit is both refreshing and complex. Subtle flavors of bread, spice, citrus, and a thirst-quenching orange honey finish.

ISLANDER PALE ALE (IPA): This West Coast IPA sweeps the senses with its intense hop bitterness and complex flavors and aromas. Medium body and maltiness.

MERMAID'S RED ALE: Well-balanced, medium- to full-bodied beer, slight caramel-roasted flavor. Well hopped to balance the malty sweetness.

IDIOT IPA: An all-natural India Pale Ale. Unfiltered, a big beer brewed with over 3 pounds of hops per barrel.

HOPPY DAZE: An unfiltered Belgian-style IPA brewed with a unique blend of European grains, a variety of hops and Belgian yeast to create an unforgetable taste down to its bitter end.

RED DEVIL: A full-bodied Imperial Red Ale with deep roasted-caramel flavors, subtle hints of chocolate, a soft hop presence and a lasting finish.

> FOR MORE BEER INFO, GO TO
WWW.CORONADOBREWINGCOMPANY.COM

HAVE A BEER WITH THE BREWER:

Sit down with Sean Farrell and a few Coronado beers:
www.sdtopbrewers.com/coronado

Shawn DeWitt is Director of Brewery Operations

Brewmaster Sean Farrell

Chef Lily Navarrette, Coronado Brewing Company

When you're the executive chef in a brewery, there are many places where you can draw inspiration. For Chef Lily Navarrette, the inspirations usually come in the morning, when she first arrives for work. "That's when I smell the many aromas of the brewing process," she says, "and it makes me think, alright, well, this will go with this and that will pair well with that." Overall, Lily finds cooking with beer to be easier than cooking with wine. "With wine, you have to reduce a lot, but with beer you can use it more like a spice. You can experiment more easily, and there's so much variety in beer that you can really play around a lot." Some of Lily's most satisfying dishes were created for San Diego Beer Week 2010. Many of the recipes she created specifically for that week were so successful that she put them on the regular menu. Among the most popular were the Coronado Brewhouse Ribs and the Grilled Salmon and Greek Salad with Orange Ave. Wit Vinaigrette, two of the great beer-inspired recipes that follow.

GRILLED SALMON AND GREEK SALAD
Serves 4

with Orange Ave. Wit Vinaigrette

Perfect Pairing: Coronado Orange Ave. Wit

FOR THE SALMON:
1¹/₂ pounds salmon fillets

FOR THE VINAIGRETTE:
2 tablespoons crumbled feta cheese
2 tablespoons fresh lemon juice
¹/₂ cup Coronado Orange Ave. Wit
¹/₂ teaspoon granulated sugar
¹/₂ teaspoon dried oregano
¹/₈ teaspoon salt
1 garlic clove, minced
¹/₄ cup olive oil

FOR THE SALAD:
¹/₄ cup artichoke hearts, chopped
¹/₄ cup black olives, sliced
12 to 24 red grape tomatoes
¹/₄ cup red onions, sliced
¹/₄ cup crumbled feta cheese
2 pounds mixed greens

1. Preheat a grill.
2. Cut salmon into 4 portions, and grill until just barely cooked through (about 3 minutes on each side). Remove from grill and cover with foil.

3. **Make the vinaigrette:** Combine all the ingredients (except the oil) in a medium bowl and whisk while adding the oil in a slow, steady stream.

4. **Prepare the salad:** Toss all the ingredients together with vinaigrette.
5. **To serve:** Place even portions of salad on each plate. Lay the cooked salmon on top.

CAJUN SEARED AHI APPETIZER

Serves 4

with Coronado Mermaid's Red Teriyaki Sauce

Perfect Pairing: Coronado Mermaid's Red

FOR THE TERIYAKI SAUCE:
$1/2$ cup fresh ginger, peeled and minced
1 medium bulb garlic, minced
1 tablespoon sesame oil
2 cups light soy sauce
1 cup pineapple juice
8 cups Coronado Mermaid's Red
$2 1/2$ cups dark brown sugar
$1/4$ cup cornstarch

FOR THE COLESLAW:
1 green cabbage, finely sliced
1 carrot, peeled and shredded
$1/4$ cup red cabbage, shredded
$1/2$ cup mayonnaise
$1/4$ cup pineapple juice
3 teapoons celery seed
2 tablespoons whole-grain mustard
Salt and pepper to taste

FOR THE AHI:
2 pounds ahi
$1/4$ cup Blackened Red Fish Magic (or your favorite fish rub)
2 tablespoons canola or peanut oil

FOR THE GARNISH:
1 cup teriyaki sauce (recipe above)
$1/4$ cup pickled ginger

1. Make the teriyaki sauce: In a medium pan, sauté the ginger and garlic in the sesame oil until lightly browned. Add the soy sauce, pineapple juice, and beer. Bring the mixture to a boil, add the brown sugar, return to a boil, add the cornstarch, and stir to thicken. Remove from the heat and cool in ice bath.

2. Make the coleslaw: Mix together all the ingredients and season with salt and pepper.
3. Make the ahi: Rub the fish with the Blackened Red Fish Magic or other rub. In a hot sauté pan, heat the oil to very hot and sear the ahi on both sides (about 90 seconds each side). Let it cool before cutting into thin slices.
4. To serve: Put the coleslaw mix on a plate, lay slices of ahi over it, and top with pickled ginger. Serve with the teriyaki sauce in a small dish on the side, and garnish the plate with toasted sesame seeds or fried wontons.

55

CORONADO BBQ BREWHOUSE RIBS   Serves 4

FOR THE RUB:
1 1/3 cups brown sugar
2 tablespoons black pepper
4 pounds baby back ribs (2 large racks)
8 cups Coronado Golden

FOR THE SAUCE:
1/2 cup ginger, peeled and minced
1/4 cup serrano peppers, diced
2 cups yellow onion, diced
4 cups Coronado Mermaid's Red
2 cups chile sauce (such as Red Rooster
   or Tio Pepe)
1 1/3 cups brown sugar
4 cups BBQ sauce (use your favorite)

1. Preheat the oven to 350°F.
2. Mix together the brown sugar and black pepper. Crust the ribs with the mixture and place them in a baking dish with the beer, cover with foil, and place in the oven for 2 hours, or until they are tender. Let them cool.
3. Make the sauce: Braise the ginger, serranos, and onions in the Mermaid's Red beer until very soft. Remove from the heat and purée the mixture in a food processor.
4. In a separate bowl combine the chile sauce, brown sugar, and BBQ sauce. Add the ginger mixture and blend all the ingredients together.
5. Coat the ribs with the ginger sauce and grill them on low heat until warmed.
6. To serve: Cut the ribs into 4 portions, spoon more ginger sauce over them, and serve with your favorite side, such as mashed potatoes, coleslaw, or grilled veggies.

DOWNTOWN JOHNNY BROWN'S

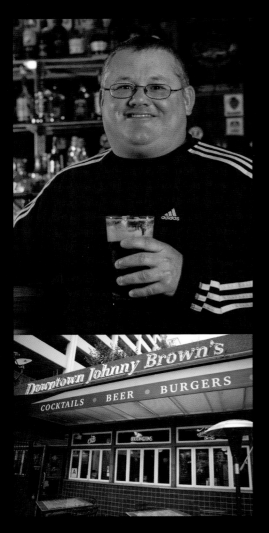

UNTIL RECENTLY, THERE HAVE BEEN RELATIVELY FEW BARS IN DOWNTOWN SAN DIEGO that have dedicated themselves to a serious craft beer lineup. The irony of this fact has not escaped the brewing community, most of whom are brewing world-class beer within 10 or 15 miles from downtown. There is one place, however, that's been recognized as one of downtown's craft beer leaders: Downtown Johnny Brown's (DTJB's).

Many would say that DTJB's owner, Todd Alexander, is doing his "civic duty" by actively promoting San Diego craft brews. This is particularly fitting, because DTJB's is tucked away in a corner of the Civic Center's courtyard, where it shares space with theaters, concert halls, and various office buildings. "For me, I think it's better for my community, for our environment, for us to keep our money and our resources here in San Diego," Todd explains. "So, if we can get the best pint of beer from something that's brewed within our city, it's better than shipping it in from of thousands of miles away."

When John Brown opened his bar in 1986, there was no such thing as a "San Diego beer scene." (It would be three years before Karl Strauss was founded.) Back then, Todd worked at DTJB's as a busboy, then a bartender, and eventually as a manager. When John decided to retire in 2004, Todd knew he'd found his calling. "I'd always wanted my own place," Todd remembers, "and it turned out to be a good opportunity."

Since he's become an owner, Todd has seen great, positive changes in awareness about San Diego beer. "It's exponential,"

Left (top): DTJB's owner, Todd Alexander; (bottom): The bar is tucked away in the Civic Center courtyard.

Above (left): Happy patrons at the bar; (right): DTJB's signature fish tacos.

he says. "When I took over and joined the San Diego Brewers Guild as an allied member, there were three members: Johnny Brown's, Liar's Club, and O'Brien's. And that was it. Now I think there's more than fifteen allied members, in just five or six years." Like his fellow beer advocates, Todd is also jazzed by the innovation and creativity he sees in the brewing community. "The diversity is really exciting and really great," Todd explains. "There are so many breweries out there doing so many things — I mean, every conceivable niche that you can think of is being filled. And that's continuing to be expanded all the time. Lightning, they're pushing the extremes of lager — what Lost Abbey is doing with sours is incredible — the creativity that's out there, that's truly exciting."

GREEN FLASH BREWING CO.

{TAP FACTS}

- Began pouring:
  2002
- Brewery size:
  45,000 square feet
- Production per year:
  25,000 barrels
- Recent awards:
  More than 30 medals
  in last five years,
  including Green Flash
  Stout (silver WBC)

There are certain names that just keep coming up whenever you ask San Diego brewers about the peers and colleagues they admire most. One of those names is Green Flash. The consensus among the professional brewing community is that Chuck Silva and his brewing team are consistently making some of the region's most creative and exciting beers.

Word about Green Flash has spread like wildfire among craft beer fans as well — the brewery

Cofounders Lisa and Mike Hinkley

is one of the fastest-growing in the region. (Of course, 30 medals from national and international competitions in the past five years has probably enhanced their popularity as well.) "We've been back-ordered for three years," explains Mike Hinkley, Green Flash cofounder and owner, with wife Lisa. "And it all comes back to the beer. Our crew makes really exceptional beer here."

Mike and Lisa didn't come to brewing through the usual channels. "We owned a local pub and got into the craft beer scene from a retailer's perspective,"

West Coast IPA
rolls through the
bottling line.

Lisa Hinkley on the Green Flash Name: "It basically comes from our backyard, where we used to sit staring at the sunset. We'd see people looking at the ocean with binoculars, and we'd ask them what they were looking for. They said they were hoping to see the 'green flash,' and we hadn't heard of that before. So when it came time to name the brewery, we thought that would be fun. It represents the coast and San Diego."

Mike explains. "We might be the only brewery founders in the whole country who never brewed their own homebrew batch of beer! But we can spend two hours in a bottle shop. We just don't have the patience for homebrewing," Mike says with a smile. "But we do appreciate the homebrewers and everything that they do. It's really how the whole craft beer movement got started."

Lisa says that their vision for the company has "actually changed a lot since we first started in 2002. We started out trying to make an Extra Pale Ale. We wanted it to be a little lower in alcohol, and with lots of hops and lots of flavor. We thought we'd sell it at grocery stores in San Diego." The Hinkleys, however, didn't expect the intense competition and pressure that comes with a mainstream business. "Everything we originally thought wound up changing," Lisa explains. "Then we made a West Coast IPA. It was intended to be a benchmark of what a West Coast IPA was. Real hoppy style and complex in its hoppiness. Yakima Valley hops and Simcoe hops. It was the beer that we liked to drink best. Making that beer really

changed the course of what we do."

Mike and Lisa credit much of their success to the considerable talents of champion brewmaster Chuck Silva. Since 2004, Chuck has developed the Green Flash "identity" and signature styles for the company. "Our identity is characterized a lot by the hoppy beers we make," Chuck explains. "We're definitely putting a lot of flavor into all our beers, even the lighter, sessionable [lower alcohol; able to

Looking back on their early days, Mike and Lisa think about why the San Diego brewing scene exploded the way it has: "I think it was timing and people. It really came together in '96, '97, and '98, when Stone, and AleSmith, and Ballast Point started making beers. And there was a great collection of brewers working at those companies. And the initial beers that they started out with were exceptional. So, for the competition, you had to really be a great beer to get put on tap." Chuck adds his unique perspective: "I always point to the fact that we've had a core group of great brewmasters in San Diego. We've brought our craft up considerably over the years — me for thirteen years, Tomme Arthur at Lost Abbey for fifteen or sixteen, Paul Segura over at Karl Strauss, and many others. All these guys have been brewing here for a long time."

Before 2011, Green Flash was bursting at the seams — literally. Even after they tripled their Vista factory space, they still didn't have room to supply the demand. So, they built an entirely new space in Mira Mesa, one that provided major new square footage and lots of room to grow. Not only does the new location offer a super venue for tasting, it also means Chuck and the Hinkleys can expand their production and the kinds of beers they produce. "I'm looking forward to being able to bottle some of our seasonal beers and special releases. The things that we couldn't make available before," Chuck explains. "I think now we'll be able to offer more of the special things our fans have been asking for."

drink multiple servings] ones." Chuck goes on to say that the popularity of his hoppy brews is based on the fact that "they're so rich in flavor but still very drinkable." Chuck has incorporated his love for hops into some of the Belgian styles he does as well. Le Freak, for example, is what happens when a Belgian Trippel joins forces with an American Imperial IPA.

BREWER'S NOTES

WEST COAST IPA: This West Coast–style India Pale Ale is extravagantly hopped, full flavored, medium-bodied, and copper colored.

HOP HEAD RED ALE: Resinous hop character and bitterness balance the rich caramel malt base.

IMPERIAL I.P.A.: San Diego–style IPA, as it has come to be known by many, is super-hoppy, high gravity, yet highly quaffable ale.

DOUBLE STOUT: Golden naked oats mashed with dark crystal and robust roasted malts create a luscious black brew with a satin-smooth finish. Layering UK Target hops throughout the boil adds a pleasant, earthy complexity while higher fermentation temperatures enhance overall flavor with fruity esters. Big, bold, flavorful and complex.

BARLEYWINE STYLE ALE: Rich, estery brew with toffee notes and citrus hop flavors layered throughout. Enjoy it now or lay it down for aging to see how the flavors of each vintage evolve.

LE FREAK: Belgian-style IPA. Zesty brew with enticing American hops and Belgian yeast aromatics that lead you to delicious malts and a complex layering of hop flavors.

TRIPPEL BELGIAN STYLE ALE: Rich pale malt flavors provide a solid base for zesty Styrian Golding and Czech Saaz hopping. Trappist ale yeast contributes the fruity, spicy profile of classic, monk-brewed, Belgian ales. Luscious, fiery, golden brew is a contemporary rendition of traditional Belgian Trippel.

GRAND CRU: Our Belgian–style Strong Dark Ale is inspired by traditional Abbey Ales to deliver the richest of malt flavors but with a slightly elevated hopping and increased complexity given from two different yeast strains.

SUMMER SAISON: Unfiltered golden farmhouse ale, brewed with orange curaçao, ginger, and grains of paradise.

> FOR MORE BEER INFO,
GO TO WWW.GREENFLASHBREW.COM

HAVE A BEER WITH THE BREWER:

Sit down with Chuck Silva and a few Green Flash beers:

www.sdtopbrewers.com/greenflash

65

Chef Jeff Rossman, Terra American Bistro

One of San Diego's star chefs, Jeff Rossman has been incorporating beers into his recipes for a long time. He's also created many special beer dinners at his popular restaurant, Terra, where he has showcased the region's great brews. Jeff is all about using and supporting local suppliers — whether they are organic farmers, local winemakers, or local brewers. The recipe that follows was done in collaboration with Green Flash for Beer Week 2010, where it became a particular favorite of Green Flash's brewmaster, Chuck Silva. Jeff was inspired to use the barleywine with his flan because he loved the fact that it's "hoppy but it has a really nice caramel essence to it."

GREEN FLASH TRIPPEL-CURED SALMON   Serves 6

with Smoked-Onion Flan and Barleywine Syrup

Perfect Pairing: Green Flash Barleywine

FOR THE CURE:
1 tablespoon fennel seed
1 teaspoon coriander seed, toasted and
    ground
3 bay leaves
2 star anise
2 tablespoons kosher salt
¼ cup granulated sugar
¼ cup Green Flash Trippel
1 pound salmon

FOR THE FLAN:
¼ yellow onion
2 cups heavy cream
1 sprig fresh thyme
1 teaspoon fresh thyme leaves
6 large eggs
1¼ teaspoons kosher salt
¼ teaspoon freshly ground black pepper

FOR THE SYRUP:
Yields ¾ cup
1 (22-ounce) bottle Green Flash Barleywine
½ cup granulated sugar
1 sprig fresh thyme

1. Make the cure: Combine all the ingredients except the salmon in a mixing bowl.

2. Place a piece of plastic wrap, long enough to wrap the fish, on a clean cutting board. Pour the mixture from the bowl over the fish, being careful that the liquid doesn't run all over. Wrap the fish tightly with plastic wrap, then wrap it again with an additional piece of wrap.

3. Place the wrapped fish in a shallow casserole dish, put a baking sheet directly on top of the fish, and then place a heavy item or two on top of the baking sheet to weight down the fish. Refrigerate for at least 24 hours, but no longer than 48 hours.

4. Make the flan: Preheat oven to 325°F.

5. In a tabletop or standard smoker, follow the manufacturer's instructions and smoke the onion at 175°F for at least 2 hours.

6. In a medium saucepot, combine the cream and thyme and heat until just boiling.

7. In a medium bowl, separate the eggs and reserve the whites for another use. Temper the yolks with the cream mixture by adding it slowly and whisking as you go. Add the smoked onion and thyme leaves. Put the mixture into a blender, purée until smooth and and season with salt and pepper.

8. Spray six (4-ounce) ramekins with cooking spray. Pour the flan mixture into the ramekins and place them in a casserole dish. Fill the casserole dish with enough hot water to come halfway up the sides of the ramekins. Bake for about 1 hour, or until set. Let cool, then refrigerate for at least 4 hours.

9. Make the syrup: In a medium saucepot, combine all ingredients and bring to a boil. Reduce heat and simmer for about 30 minutes, or until a syrupy consistency is reached. Cool and reserve.

10. To serve: Unwrap the salmon and rinse off all the ingredients. Cut into paper-thin slices and reserve. Unmold a flan onto a plate and lay three or four slices of salmon next to — or resting on — the flan. Using a spoon, drizzle some of the barleywine syrup over the entire dish. Garnish with fried leeks, sea salt, and fresh parlsey.

HAMILTON'S TAVERN

TO THE UNTRAINED EYE, IT ALL LOOKS CASUALLY THROWN TOGETHER. There's the pool table and the shuffleboard table, the dark wood booths, the neon beer logos, the flat-screen TV, and beer posters and graphics everywhere. But this is no haphazard collection of paraphernalia. This is Hamilton's Tavern, and it's Scot Blair's vision of what a perfect neighborhood bar should be. Because he has such a passion for beer and a drive to do things right, Hamilton's is truly Scot's masterpiece.

Back in the 1990s, Scot was a homebrewer who loved going to Liar's Club, Live Wire, and O'Brien's for good beers. He was a longtime North Park resident who noticed that his area had "a lot of cool places, but not a lot of cool places that cared about beer — it wasn't the focus of what they did." Scot decided that he wanted to create his idea of the perfect beer bar. He'd always been a fan of Sparky's on 30th Street, which had been around since Prohibition, and he'd been telling his friends for years that he wanted to "buy that bar some day." When Sparky's went up for sale in 2005, Scot and his partner investor seized the opportunity and reopened it as Hamilton's

Above: Scot Blair; below (left): GM Dennis Borlek is also the talent behind Hamilton's signature house-made sausages.

tavern. "I knew exactly what I was going to do," he recalls. "I had said from the beginning, 'I don't care if I go bankrupt doing what I want to do.' I said, 'I'm gonna do this — and people will either like it or not.' Well, people liked it!"

Soon after the new bar opened, neighborhood beer-lover Dennis Borlek became a regular. As he remembers it, "Blair and I just started talking about beer. First it was one night a week. Then two nights a week. Then three. Then four. And always well, well into the morning." This turned out to be the beginning of a beautiful friendship. Today, Dennis is the general manager of Hamilton's and also a partner in Scot's two other neighborhood bars: Small Bar and Eleven. Dennis says that

Hamilton's ceiling houses the hundreds of tap handles that showcase the tavern's amazing variety of beer offerings.

he and Scot share the same ideas about what a great bar should be. In their opinion, a bar shouldn't be about promoting snobbishness or exclusivity for connoisseurs. "It's about getting the guy who's open to trying new things — it's about that guy walking out the door at the end of the night having tried five beers he's never had before." "It's about 'converting' and giving people options," Scot adds. "It's not about being an elitist a**hole about it. We never say, 'oh, you drink Budweiser? Oh, no. Get outta here.' It's about, 'here's a Heineken, but let me also give you four other things to try first.'"

The bar's reputation for great selection and hard-to-find brews has spread quickly in recent years. Scot and Dennis have worked hard to build strong relationships with brewers — and that helps when a very limited release is made available. "With some of the beers ..." Scot explains, "there are only 10 kegs for all of California." Clearly, the Scot Blair formula for the "perfect bar" is working: Hamilton's — along with its sister bars — has more craft beer flowing through its taps than any other neighborhood bar in San Diego.

HESS BREWING

IT'S MANY THE HOMEBREWER'S DREAM: start small, making handcrafted batches of great beer in your garage or backyard. Develop and hone your recipes until you have them just right and then take the leap into the world of professional brewing. Well, Mike Hess, owner and founder of Hess Brewing, is livin' the dream.

Mike had been homebrewing for about 15 years when he decided to take it to the next level. As he explains it, he was motivated by a number of factors: "Part of it was a long-time desire to be a pro brewer," Mike says. "And then desire finally met up with opportunity." Mike had always assumed there would be a large barrier to entry — he thought, in order to make it, a new brewery would need a lot of capital and equipment and would have to produce on a large scale. Then he found out that "nano-brewing" was actually a viable option. "One of my friends showed me an article about nano-brewing," Mike recalls. "I saw what folks were doing, and I thought we could do it, too. So we did."

Despite the fact that he was an active homebrewer for many years, Mike admits sheepishly that he didn't really grow out of the "official" homebrew community. "I'm probably the oddball," he says. "I didn't plug in at all to any of the San Diego homebrew scene. Though I've gotten a lot of support from them, I'd always intended to get involved in QUAFF, had it on

Mike Hess has finally made the leap into pro brewing.

Above (left): Tasting Room Manager, Michael Skubic, fills a growler; (right): Hess still brews 1.6 barrel batches.

my calendar, but with wife and family and businesses, it just never worked out."

Mike's latest leap, though major, still keeps things on a relatively small scale for now. Hess calls itself "San Diego's first licensed nano-brewery," which means his beers are brewed 1.6 barrels (51 gallons) at a time. Stylistically, Hess stands out from the crowd by pushing styles to their limits, while maintaining their drinkability. "I think what sets us apart is that we have a broad range of styles and can't be pigeon-holed into any overarching stylistic theme," Mike explains. "We make beers that range from Kölsch on one end to our 10% Rye Imperial Stout, Ex Umbris on the other." Mike believes he has one beer that's unique to San Diego. "It's called Grazias, which is a Vienna Cream Ale. I don't think anyone else in town is doing that." Even the growlers are a unique aspect of the brewery. The large, 2-liter bottles sport a cut-glass design with metal handles and swing tops. "Why would I spend all that time making the beer perfect, then put it in a substandard vessel?" Mike remarks. "We're trying to keep it classy and do it right the first time."

IRON FIST BREWING CO.

{TAP FACTS}

- Began pouring: 2010
- 15-barrel brewhouse
- Brewery and tasting room size: 6,000 square feet
- Production per year: 3,000 barrels
- Distribution: Partnership with Stone Brewing Co.

Most of San Diego's breweries are relatively small, and their owners often refer to their staff as "family." At Iron Fist, however, the "family" is literally family. Talented brewmaster Brandon Sieminski brews his lineup with the invaluable help of his family, including his father, Greg. His mother, Eve, works more behind the scenes, managing the business and coordinating various marketing aspects. Even Eve's parents, Edith and Les Piestrzeniewicz (affectionately known as "Grandma and Grandpa Fist"), are frequently found working the tasting room, where a considerable number of fans gather on a regular basis. (The tasting room, by the way, is decorated with framed photos of Brandon and his family.)

One of San Diego's youngest breweries is run by San Diego's youngest pro brewer. Despite his age, Brandon (who turned 21 in 2010) is no newcomer to brewing. Before starting Iron Fist, Brandon had been homebrewing for years, experimenting with styles, figuring out what he liked, and perfecting his techniques. "I guess brewing combines my two passions — cooking and science. To make good beer, you definitely have to have the science side, but you also

Brandon works a
state-of-the-art
brewhouse.

The family (left to right): Greg (father), Eve (mother), Edith (grandmother), Les (grandfather), Adrian (brother), and Brandon.

have to have the artistic part of it, like you would in the culinary arts — it has to taste good, too."

While traveling with his family in eastern Europe, Brandon had been especially inspired by the beers of Germany, Poland, and the Czech Republic. "It was that trip that first inspired me to start homebrewing," he explains. "The guys in those countries were doing a lot of lagers — definitely different from the things people are doing around here, but [with] the same idea: quality beer." With a "new-found appreciation for beer" Brandon returned to San Diego and quickly realized that he was living right in the middle of the "Napa Valley of

Beer, right in my own backyard."

When it came time to make the leap to pro brewing, Brandon just considered it a natural progression. "I had started to do only all-grain batches," he recalls. "I was encouraged because the first all-grain batch didn't suck, which was a good sign. In fact, it just kept getting better from there."

Early on in the planning stages, Brandon spent some time getting acquainted with all the styles being done in San Diego. He really loved Ballast Point's Yellowtail Pale Ale and was a big fan of oaked Stone's Arrogant Bastard. He also became a huge fan of Lost Abbey and Port Brewing, whom he

hopes his story can inspire others who dream of going bigger. "It's kind of a tale of hope for other homebrewers," he says. "If you have the dream and you pursue it, you never know what might happen."

Brandon has always had a clear vision of the beers he wants to brew. And he's also had some strong opinions on technique. "All my beers are conditioned, I never do forced carbonation," he explains. Brandon feels strongly that conditioning (allowing the beer to ferment in bottle or keg with the natural yeasts and a bit of added fermentable sugar) enhances the flavor profiles and the mouthfeel.

Clearly Brandon's approach is paying off. Pro brewers all over San Diego have already taken notice of this "young gun's" talents, and many say he's one of the county's most promising "rising stars." (Scot Blair, owner of Hamilton's Tavern, calls Brandon the "Justin Bieber of the San Diego brew scene.") Brandon laughs when he hears this. He attributes his success so far to his homebrew background, which left him free to experiment and not "be constrained" by a rigid set of rules and regulations. "I guess I had the benefit of being naïve," Brandon explains. "We didn't have the burden of knowledge that everything has to be 'just-so.' It has always been about doing what works, rather than doing things 'the way they should be done.' We don't necessarily do everything in the traditional method — the method that would be prescribed in many books. So far, we've been able to make good beer, and do it consistently, so it's worked for us."

recognized as doing "really excellent beers." It was partly due to that exposure that Brandon decided to focus a lot of his brewing on Belgian styles, which were the beers he most loved to drink. When Iron Fist first opened its doors in mid-October 2010, the beer lineup included a nice variety of Belgian-inspired beers that spanned the ranges from light and crisp to rich and bold.

Brandon was lucky to have a family that believed in his talent and was also willing to step up and help him make his dream come true. Everyone pitched in — financially and emotionally — and pledged to do their part in making Iron Fist a reality. Brandon

BREWER'S NOTES

HIRED HAND: Saison. Brewed year round. Perfectly blends malty and sour notes, with a refreshing, dry finish.

RENEGADE BLONDE: Kölsch-style Blonde Ale. When it's young, it has a crisp, malty flavor with a refreshingly bitter finish, not unlike a lager. With age, it develops a mild, fruity character, like an ale.

SPICE OF LIFE: Belgian-style Spiced Ale. We embrace the flavors and launch them into a full frontal assault of delicious bitter orange peel and grains of paradise. Beautifully smooth coriander complements the orange peel perfectly.

GOLDEN AGE: Belgian-style Golden Strong Ale. Citrusy tasting. Mesmerizing march of perfect champagne-like bubbles to the foam front draws you in. Hints of lemon, grape, and apple.

DUBBEL FISTED: Abbey-style Dubbel. Rich chocolate, caramel, and plum notes are almost too tempting for words.

VELVET GLOVE: Stout. Placid appearance and unparalleled smoothness. Rich, chocolaty espresso dominates the flavor profile, with a velvety smooth texture that will haunt your senses.

THE GAUNTLET: Imperial IPA. Seriously intense beer. The inordinate amount of hop flavor and aroma from this creamy, froth-covered liquid is enough to make this brewmaster blush.

> FOR MORE BEER INFO, GO TO
WWW.IRONFISTBREWING.COM

HAVE A BEER WITH THE BREWER:

Sit down with Brandon Sieminski and a few Iron Fist beers:

www.sdtopbrewers.com/ironfist

Mike Campbell
When Iron Fist first opened its doors in Vista, California, Mike Campbell quickly became one of its first loyal fans. Since then, Mike has become an honorary member of the Iron Fist team — he helps out at the brewery in whatever ways he can. He frequently contributes a slow cooker full of his delicious tri-tip, which he serves to the Iron Fist crew on slider rolls. When asked for their favorite recipe to include here, Brandon, Eve, and Greg didn't have to think twice: so here it is.

VELVET GLOVE PUB SLIDERS

Serves 8 to 10

Perfect Pairing: Iron Fist Renegade Blonde

1 untrimmed tri-tip roast (2 to 4 pounds)
2 (750-ml) bottles Iron Fist Velvet Glove Imperial Stout
1 large yellow onion, sliced
10 to 15 cloves of garlic, crushed
$\frac{1}{2}$ cup soy sauce
2 tablespoons Worcestershire sauce
2 tablespoons good-quality balsamic vinegar
3 cups vegetable stock
Freshly ground pepper to taste
Cheese slices, optional

1. Place the tri-tip in a large, sealable plastic bag with 1 bottle of Velvet Glove Imperial Stout. Marinate for a minimum of 6 hours, or overnight in the refrigerator.
2. Place the marinated meat (not the liquid from the marinade) in a slow cooker. Add the second bottle of Velvet Glove, the onions, garlic, soy sauce, Worcestershire sauce, and balsamic vinegar. Add the vegetable stock until the meat is covered.
3. Cook on low setting for 8 hours or on high setting for 5 to 6 hours. The meat will shred easily when fully cooked.
4. To serve: Spoon the shredded meat onto slider buns, sesame rolls, or your favorite bread or roll. Top with cheese, if desired. Great with a small dish of "jus" from the slow cooker for dipping, a variety of mustards, pickles, and chips or crackers.

KARL STRAUSS BREWING COMPANY

{TAP FACTS}

- Began pouring: 1989

- Brewery size: 25,000 square feet

- Production per year: 42,000 barrels

- Brews more than 30 different beers a year

- Karl Strauss beers can be found in more than 2,500 bars, restaurants, and retailers throughout Southern California

- Recent awards: Red Trolley Ale (gold GABF; gold WBC)

Before there was anything even remotely called a "craft beer community" in San Diego, there was Karl Strauss Brewing Company. When cofounders Chris Cramer and Matt Rattner first opened their doors in 1989, the city had been without a local brewery for more than 50 years. It took a lot of guts — and a great dedication to the idea of locally made, handcrafted beer — but that's how San Diego began its most recent beermaking renaissance.

Chris and Matt had been inspired by a great brewpub Chris found while traveling in Australia after college graduation. When he returned to San Diego, the two graduates decided to try their hand at opening their own brewery. Luckily, Chris had a cousin who happened to be a master brewer. His name? Karl Strauss. It was with Karl's guidance and knowledge that the company's first beer recipes were developed and brewed (in 10-gallon batches).

Cofounders Chris Cramer (left) and Matt Rattner

Of course, since the 1980s, San Diego's beer scene has exploded with all kinds of breweries and styles of beer. Through it all, though, Karl Strauss Brewing Company has remained an icon — a shining example of how a craft brewery can grow, and still remain a vital, exciting, and relevant member of the beer scene.

Native San Diegan and brewmaster, Paul Segura, like Karl Strauss Brewing Company itself, has a long and rich history of brewing in San Diego. He sees his mission as twofold: First, he strives to brew a selection of beers that will provide something for every palate and taste. "At each of our brewpubs, we have ten taps," Paul explains, "so there's always something that's hoppy, something that's dark, ales, lagers, Hefeweizen — something for anybody who walks in the door. We also try to have our beers be representative of the style from which they came."

The second part of Paul's mission is to stay creative and to offer his patrons new brews that are different and exciting. "Sometimes we'll do something crazy, throw something new in there, and brew something that no one has ever done before. We like to push the envelope, too."

Recently, Karl Strauss Brewing Company launched a series of "big beers" to be available in 22-ounce bombers. "That's in addition to the rotating seasonal beers that we do in the 12-ounce bottles," he explains. "So every other month, we're doing a high gravity, big beer that true beer aficionados will enjoy." So far, Paul's lineup has included Belgian

The brewpub always offers a great menu with an exciting lineup of beers on tap.

IPAs, an Imperial Pilsner, a double IPA, and Karl Strauss's 22nd Anniversary Ale, which is an oak-aged vanilla Russian Imperial Stout. Paul says he's got a bunch of other new ideas for types of beer he wants to brew. Among them are more sour beers, more oak-aged beers, and beers aged in other kinds of barrels. "Like everyone else in San Diego, we're going to continue to innovate and push the envelope. We want to continue to try to be the pioneers."

The recent boom in San Diego's beer business

has generated lots of activity for Karl Strauss Brewing Company, and Paul is excited to be a part of it. "To see San Diego go from, basically, just Karl Strauss to all of these different breweries, making all of these great beers, is really pretty cool. There are a lot of other brewers in San Diego that got their start at Karl Strauss — I can name five or six of them off the top of my head, and that's really gratifying." Paul is also aware of the healthy competition and the "competitive camaraderie" that's an integral part of being a San Diego brewer. In many ways,

the brewers have created such high standards for themselves that everyone in the brewing community feels a responsibility to live up to the city's impressive reputation.

Today, Karl Strauss brews more than 30 different beers a year, including their famous Red Trolley Ale, which won gold at both the 2010 Great American Beer Festival and the 2010 World Beer Cup. As of 2011, Karl Strauss beers can be found in more than 2,500 bars, restaurants, supermarkets, and other retailers throughout Southern California.

BREWER'S NOTES

RED TROLLEY ALE: Copper colored. Sweet toffee and caramel aroma. Undertones of plums, dates, and raisins. Finishes smooth with a lingering sweetness.

TOWER 10 IPA: Golden orange. Vibrant floral aroma. Zesty grapefruit and tangerine hop flavors. Finishes bone-dry with a lingering bitterness.

PINTAIL PALE ALE: Amber color. Ruby red grapefruit aroma. Floral and citrus hop flavors. Finishes dry with a hint of caramel malt.

FULLSUIT BELGIAN BROWN: Russet brown. Smell of sweet coffee. Toasted and nutty malt character. Peppery Belgian yeast notes. Smooth and spicy finish.

WHISTLER IMPERIAL PILS: Pale golden. Aroma of fresh cut grass. Toasted malts and spicy Noble hop flavors. Finishes crisp and dry.

BIG BARREL DOUBLE IPA: Honey colored. Tropical nose. Passion fruit, mango, pineapple hop character. Assertive bitterness. Dry finish.

> FOR MORE BEER INFO, GO TO WWW.KARLSTRAUSS.COM

HAVE A BEER WITH THE BREWER:

Sit down with Paul Segura and a few Karl Strauss beers:

www.sdtopbrewers.com/karlstrauss

Executive Chef Gunther Emathinger, Karl Strauss Brewing Company

As a chef, Gunther Emathinger finds beer a challenge to cook with — but it's a good challenge. He likes to say, "Incorporating beer into recipes is a fun adventure. Beer is very diverse, and there are so many different flavors to work with, it makes it really fun." His main goal, as he tells it, is always to come up with recipes that "make the beer better and make the food better. Coming up with the perfect match is something we all strive for every time." Gunther tends to use beer in his kitchen in many of the same ways that others use wine. He sautés with it, deglazes pans with it, uses it in stocks and batters, and also in cold dressings. "The one thing you have to watch out for in beer is the bitterness," he explains. "This can sometimes be a plus, but can also be a handicap. We use bitter beers in steamed mussels, for example, where the bitterness really helps to cut the richness of a buttery sauce." A few of Gunther's great beer-inspired creations are included in the following pages, including one of his all-time personal favorites, his Black Garlic Fondue. "It's very unusual, and the flavors are wonderful. Black garlic is a fermented garlic that's got a real sweetness and a fruit flavor to it. It's absolutely fantastic with our Red Trolley Ale. A combination to die for!"

BLACK GARLIC FONDUE   Serves 4

Perfect Pairing: Karl Strauss Red Trolley Ale

FOR THE BLACK GARLIC:
½ cup Karl Strauss Red Trolley Ale
½ cup water
1 bulb black garlic *(Black garlic is available at specialty retailers such as Whole Foods and Bristol Farms as well as online).*

FOR THE FONDUE:
1 tablespoon olive oil
1 tablespoon shallots, finely diced
2 tablespoons roasted red bell pepper strips (canned), drained and coarsely chopped
1 tablespoon fresh basil, coarsely chopped
1 tablespoon fresh parsley, coarsely chopped
5 ounces cambazola cheese, divided: 2 ounces for the sauce and the remaining 3 ounces for the fondue (may substitute with Maytag blue or any other triple cream blue cheese)
½ cup heavy cream
Salt and freshly ground pepper to taste

1. Prepare the black garlic: Combine the Red Trolley Ale and water in a small sauce pan and bring to a boil. Add the whole bulb of black garlic and simmer for about 3 minutes. Remove from heat and let cool in the cooking liquid. Remove the garlic from the liquid, and reserve the cooking liquid. Peel the garlic cloves and reserve.
2. Preheat the oven to 375°F.
3. Make the fondue: Heat the olive oil in a medium sauté pan. Add the shallots and sauté on medium heat until they are soft and translucent. Add the roasted pepper strips, basil, and parsley, and sauté for 30 seconds.

4. Add a ¼ cup of reserved cooking liquid, bring it to a boil, and let it reduce by half.
5. Add the 2 ounces of cheese and the heavy cream to the reduced cooking liquid, and bring it back to a boil. Reduce by a third, stirring often.
6. Once the sauce is smooth and creamy, add the black garlic cloves, and season with freshly ground pepper and salt to taste.
7. Pour the sauce into an ovenproof shallow dish, approximately 8 inches in diameter and 1-inch deep.
8. Place the remaining cheese atop the sauce in the center of the dish and bake in the oven for approximately 2 to 3 minutes until the cheese begins to soften. Remove from the oven and serve immediately. Serve with crusty French or grilled sourdough bread.

WOODIE GOLD
DRUNKEN SHRIMP

Serves 2

Perfect Pairing: Karl Strauss Pintail Pale Ale

1 tablespoon olive oil
$\frac{1}{2}$ pound raw shrimp, 21/25 count, peeled
   and deveined
1 tablespoon fresh garlic, minced
1 tablespoon fresh shallots, minced
$\frac{1}{2}$ cup Karl Strauss Woodie Gold
1 tablespoon fresh basil, chopped
1 tablespoon fresh parsley, chopped
2 tablespoons fresh tomatoes, diced
$\frac{1}{2}$ cup heavy cream
$\frac{1}{2}$ tablespoon Cajun seasoning
2 tablespoons unsalted butter
Salt and pepper to taste

1. In a large skillet, heat the olive oil to hot.
2. Carefully add the shrimp. Let the shrimp brown slightly on one side (about 30 to 45 seconds) then turn them over.
3. Add the garlic and the shallots and sauté until both are light brown.
4. Deglaze the pan with the beer, and reduce the liquid by half.
5. Add the basil, parsley, tomatoes, heavy cream, and Cajun spice.
6. Reduce the sauce by about a third, to a creamy consistency.
7. Turn off the heat, add the butter, and mix until all the butter is incorporated. Adjust seasoning with salt and pepper.
8. To serve: This dish is great with mashed potatoes and wilted spinach. Arrange shrimp on top of or around your side dishes. Spoon some sauce over the shrimp.

RED TROLLEY GRILLED PORK CHOPS   Serves 4

Perfect Pairing: Karl Strauss Red Trolley Ale or Fullsuit Belgian Brown

FOR THE PORK CHOPS:
1 1/2 cups light brown sugar
1/2 cup salt
4 cups Karl Strauss Red Trolley Ale
4 (8-ounce) center cut pork chops,
   frenched (rib ends trimmed)

**FOR THE SPICY CHINESE MUSTARD
   SAUCE:**
6 tablespoons Chinese hot mustard
   powder
2 tablespoons water
1/2 cup heavy cream
2 tablespoons honey

FOR THE GLAZE:
1 3/4 cups light soy sauce
3/4 cup light brown sugar
1/4 cup seasoned rice vinegar
2 teaspoons cider vinegar
2 tablespoons sweet chile sauce
3 tablespoons sriracha sauce *(available
   in supermarket Asian food aisles)*
1/2 teaspoon red chile flakes
2 tablespoons white sesame seeds
2 tablespoons black sesame seeds
1 1/2 tablespoons fresh basil, chopped
1 tablespoon fresh cilantro, chopped
2 tablespoons fresh ginger, peeled and
   minced
3 tablespoons cornstarch
1/4 cup water

1. Brine the pork chops: In a medium bowl, combine the brown sugar, salt, and the Red Trolley Ale. Mix until the sugar and salt are dissolved. Add the pork chops, submerging them completely, and refrigerate for 3 to 6 hours. Turn the chops every couple of hours.

2. Make the mustard sauce: In a small bowl, mix all the ingredients thoroughly. Allow the sauce to rest for at least 15 minutes to let the flavors develop.

3. Make the glaze: In a medium stockpot, add all the ingredients except the cornstarch and water and bring to a boil. In a small bowl, mix the cornstarch with the water. Add the cornstarch mixture to the boiling glaze in a slow stream, stirring constantly. Boil the glaze for 30 seconds, remove from the heat, and keep hot for serving.

4. Grill the pork chops: Remove the pork chops from the brine, rinse them with water, and pat them dry with a paper towel. Grill the chops on a medium to hot grill, approximately 12 to 15 minutes per side.

5. To serve: Accompany with your favorite vegetable and a potato side dish. Place the veggies and potatoes in the center of the plate and lean the pork chops against the potatoes and veggies. Ladle a quarter cup of the soy ginger glaze around the plate and over the chops, and then drizzle 2 tablespoons of the spicy mustard sauce around the plate.

BEERAMISU

Serves 8 to 10

Perfect Pairing: Karl Strauss Oatmeal Stout or 22nd Anniversary Ale

FOR THE BEERAMISU:
1 cup cream cheese
8 ounces mascarpone cheese
1 tablespoon vanilla extract
1½ cups powdered sugar
1 pint heavy whipping cream
3 cups Karl Strauss Oatmeal Stout
40 ladyfingers, divided

FOR THE CHOCOLATE SHARD GARNISH:
8 ounces white chocolate
2 tablespoons freshly ground coffee beans
Unsweetened cocoa powder, for dusting

1. In a large bowl, combine the cream cheese, mascarpone, vanilla, and 1 cup of powdered sugar. Beat the mixture until it is smooth and creamy.

2. In a separate bowl, beat the heavy whipping cream with the remaining powdered sugar until stiff peaks form.

3. Gently fold the mascarpone mixture into the whipped cream until just combined.

4. Pour the beer into a medium shallow dish. Lightly dip the ladyfingers in beer, coating both sides.

5. Arrange 20 of the dipped ladyfingers on the bottom of a 13-inch x 9-inch baking dish and spread half the cream mixture on top.

6. Place the remaining lightly soaked ladyfingers atop the cream and cover with the second half of the cream mixture. Cover with plastic wrap and refrigerate overnight.

7. Make the chocolate shards: In a double boiler on low heat, melt the white chocolate until smooth. Remove from heat and spread the melted chocolate onto a parchment paper-lined baking sheet to about a ⅛-inch thickness.

8. Sprinkle the coffee grounds over the still-soft chocolate and refrigerate until the chocolate hardens.

9. Remove the chocolate from the refrigerator and break it into irregularly shaped shards. Reserve in dry, cool place.

10. To serve: Remove the well-chilled beeramisu from the refrigerator and dust the top generously with the cocoa powder. Cut into squares. Stick a chocolate shard into each square of beeramisu, and serve. It's even better when you serve this with a drizzle of your favorite caramel sauce and/or chocolate sauce!

LIGHTNING BREWERY

{TAP FACTS}

- Began pouring: 2006
- Brewery size:
  5,500 square feet
- Production per year:
  1,000 barrels
- Recent awards:
  Elemental Pilsner
  (gold and third best
  of show CA State Fair
  2010); Amber Ale
  (gold LA International
  Commercial Beer
  Competition 2010);
  Old Tempest Ale (gold
  CA State Fair 2010).

Like many great and interesting things, brewing is both an art and a science. On the surface, making beer seems fairly simple. After all, it's really just the combination of four basic elements: grain, water, hops, and yeast. Of course, it's how those elements are combined that defines the art.

Lightning Brewery owner, founder, and brewmaster Jim Crute is a scientist by training and a beer lover at heart. It's his unique ability to combine scientific principles and experimentation to his beermaking that enables him to create some of San Diego's most unique and interesting beers.

Jim has been making beer in one place or another since he was in graduate school in 1982. "You have to remember that, back then, hair was big and beer was little," he quips. "And this was in upstate New York, and the

Jim Crute

beer was *very, very* little. The big [local] beer then was Genesee Cream Ale, and it was not nearly as good then as it is now." Wanting more from his beer-drinking experiences, Jim felt he had no choice but to teach himself how to make beer. So, he trotted into a nearby homebrew store, set himself up with supplies, and

Brewery staffer Scott Linnett hauls some spent grain.

went home to make his own. "The first batch of beer I made was straight from extract," he remembers. "It was kind of watery and didn't have good flavor. So I pretty much went to what's called partial mashing right away and did that for a good 15 years." Jim adds, "My motto was: if primitive man can do it, you can probably do it in your kitchen."

The next progression for Jim was all-grain brewing, which he did as he pursued a career in the San Diego biotech industry. "The company that I went to work for got purchased about six weeks after I started, and my job sort of trickled out after eighteen months. I looked around for a job, realized I wasn't going to get one in San Diego — but I didn't want to move, and my wife didn't want to move — so I decided I was going to start a business. Then I thought, 'well what do I know about other than biochemistry? Well, I know a lot about beer.'" Jim goes on to explain that many of his friends were actually relieved to hear he was switching fields. "I was involved in some pretty esoteric areas of biochemistry, and people couldn't really get wrapped around it too well. But they could understand perfectly well when I told them I was making beer. They were really happy."

Of course, there's plenty of biochemistry in beermaking. "In fact," Jim says, "you could say that the brewing industry was started by biochemistry science. Louis Pasteur was the first biochemist, and he was focused on winemaking and beer and microbiology."

The early days were filled with the usual trial and error, as Jim tried to perfect his techniques and procedures. Fortunately, there were a few key people who made themselves available to him to answer questions and provide support. "The folks at Ballast Point — specifically Yuseff [Cherney] — were really nice about answering questions for me," Jim recalls.

When Jim became serious about starting his own brewery, back around 2003–2004, he started with a thorough evaluation of the San Diego breweries that were already making their mark. "There was already a healthy microbrewery trade in San Diego; it wasn't an area without craft beer — in fact, craft beer was well known and respected. And that, actually, was a good thing, because then you don't have to make your own market that way." Jim gives a lot of credit to Karl Strauss Brewing Company for "building the concept of craft beer" and establishing a lot of San Diego's early craft beer reputation. He also gives great credit to Steve Wagner and Greg Koch of Stone Brewing Co. for expanding and enhancing that market with different styles.

"So, my feeling was, there's already a craft beer

trade in San Diego, but it's primarily focused on ales — and it's focused on beers that tend to be very strongly hopped, and there's not a lot of German-styled beers being made. So, if you kind of look at what the beer space is, there seemed to be room for more lagers and malty character beers. We decided to push in that direction."

Lagers are always more of a technical challenge — and more of a time commitment — than ales. For one thing, lagers simply take twice as long to ferment as ales. "The other issue with lager beers," Jim explains, "is that the flavors tend to be accentuated from the malt and have a very subtle yeast character. That's another way of saying if you screw something up, everybody knows it."

Jim's intuition about staking out a somewhat unique territory and making his own mark on classic styles has paid off. Lightning continues to expand its distribution and availability and has become one of San Diego's more popular breweries, especially for lagers and lighter styles. Lightning's Elemental Pilsner, for example, has consistently been a best-selling beer at Hamilton's and other high-traffic San Diego craft beer hubs. As of 2011, Jim's beers were available at more than 125 San Diego locations.

Notoriety and recognition have also come Lightning's way in recent years. Their Elemental Pilsner was the gold medal winner at the California State Fair in 2010 and was Third Best in Show. "In an area of the country where heavily hopped beers — particularly the western hopped beers — are very popular, a German-style lager did really well. And I'm really happy about that."

BREWER'S NOTES

ELEMENTAL PILSNER: Clean, crisp, and refreshing. Full-bodied. Dry and slightly bitter finish.

THUNDERWEIZEN ALE: Lots of wheat, vigorous fermentation, and completely unfiltered for a full, refreshing flavor. Hints of banana, citrus, clove, and other spices.

AMERICAN AMBER ALE: Our take on the English Extra Special Bitter, only hoppier, more malty, and higher ABV. This recipe has been largely unchanged for 25 years.

FAIR WEATHER PALE ALE: A light and smooth carbonation permeates this malty medium-bodied beer to close with a clean, slightly bitter, and lingering finish.

OLD TEMPEST ALE: Rich, smooth, and slightly spicy flavor. Unfiltered, subtle complexities enhance this bold and flavorful beer, which only gets better with age.

IONIZER LAGER: Brewed at Bock strength and filtered for clarity. Medium body and slight corn sweetness. Smooth finish.

BLACK LIGHTNING PORTER: Full-bodied with a deep, dark chocolate character. Strong, malty backbone is balanced by a healthy dose of European and American hop bitterness. Ages incredibly well (optimal temp: 50°F.), increasing in smoothness, creaminess, and chocolate character over time. We've enjoyed some that is over four years old!

FULMINATOR LAGER: Rich, flavorful, and unfiltered. Malty with hints of sherry. Medium-bodied, with a light, easy carbonation and sweet finish.

ELECTROSTATIC ALE: Our French Farmhouse Ale. Medium-bodied, unfiltered, sweet malty foundation with a touch of sourness and hints of spiciness.

> FOR MORE BEER INFO, GO TO
WWW.LIGHTNINGBREWERY.COM

HAVE A BEER WITH THE BREWER:

Sit down with Jim Crute and a few Lightning beers:

www.sdtopbrewers.com/lightning

Chef Kyle Bergman:
The Grill at The Lodge at Torrey Pines
In devising this recipe, Chef Kyle was inspired by the intense yeasty and fruity aromas of clove and banana that shine through Thunderweizen — Lightning's Hefeweizen. "Everybody does mussels in wine, and I don't see any reason why you can't do mussels in beer. Besides, I've seen it done before, particularly in Belgium. So I kind of stole the idea," Kyle admits. When he first tasted the Hef, he knew that it was the beer he wanted to do the mussels with. "You wouldn't want to use a hoppier beer, or something that's too light," he says. Kyle also thinks that Thunderweizen actually makes the mussels taste fresher: "The body, the great mouthfeel of the beer, with the little bit of sweetness does it, along with the lightness of the lemon."

THUNDERWEIZEN STEAMED MUSSELS   Serves 2

with Pancetta and Meyer Lemon Jam

Perfect Pairing: Lightning Thunderweizen

FOR THE LEMON JAM:
2 pounds Meyer lemons, cut in thick
   rounds and seeded
1 cup salt
1 cup sugar
1 pinch hot chile flakes

FOR THE MUSSELS:
1 cup pancetta, diced large
2 tablespoons butter, unsalted
2 medium shallots, cut into rings
2 pounds black mussels (washed and
   debearded)
1 cup Lightning Thunderweizen
1 cup Meyer lemon jam
2 cups parsley leaves
Salt and pepper to taste

1. Make the lemon jam: In a large bowl, combine all the ingredients. Refrigerate overnight. Give the mixture a rough chop and drain any extra liquid.

2. Make the mussels: Sauté the pancetta in half of the butter until rendered and crispy. Add the shallots and mussels and mix together.

3. Add the beer and the jam. Steam the mussels until they just open. (Hint: Remove them from the pan as they open, because they will cook at different rates. Then add all the cooked ones back to finish.) Discard any mussels that do not fully open.

4. Add parsley and remaining butter, season with salt and pepper, and serve hot.

LIVE WIRE

THERE ARE ONLY A FEW BAR OWNERS WHO CAN TRULY SAY THAT THEY WITNESSED THE BIRTH OF SAN DIEGO'S CRAFT BEER MOVEMENT, and Sam Chammas is one of them. Sam is the owner of Live Wire on El Cajon Boulevard in North Park, one of San Diego's oldest and most popular craft beer bars.

Many members of the craft beer community credit Live Wire with incubating the whole San Diego beer scene. "It's kind of our claim to fame," explains Sam. "We really didn't even know it was happening as it was happening, but we were a big part of it."

When the bar first opened in 1992, Sam and his longtime business partner Joe Austin had a clear vision of what they wanted in a beer bar. For one thing, they wanted to remain loyal to craft beers and microbrews — they didn't offer Budweiser. As Sam tells it, they thought, "Let's create a bar that's [got] just the beers that we like. At that time, Sam Adams was new. Sierra Nevada was new. Anchor and Red Hook, those were the big players at that time. But it was also the beginning of the local scene."

Initially, the local scene was fairly small — basically, it was Karl Strauss. It wasn't until the mid-90s that Stone, AleSmith, and Ballast Point

Owner Sam Chammas witnessed the birth of San Diego's craft beer explosion.

Live Wire has long been a North Park original.

entered the fray, to be followed soon after by Coronado and Pizza Port. At this same time, local music was also thriving. Sam remembers that "rad bands like Inch, Rocket from the Crypt, and Lucy's Fur Coat dominated North Park, and local musicians hung out here and they drank local beers."

It took some guts for Sam and Joe to hold fast to their dedication to craft beer. "Live Wire was a pioneer, yes, but in the late 1990s, we weren't crazy busy. You've got to remember, this was at a time when there was a big cocktail craze — martinis and cosmos and all that." Still, when they opened, they had 14 taps ("14 kick-ass beers" as Sam says), only pints, and nothing in a bottle. Some people were not happy with the bar's lack of mainstream offerings, and Sam would often have to defuse rants from customers who were outraged that no Bud was available. When he was called a "beer snob," he would say, "No, we are just about good beer. You can get Bud anywhere."

A lot has changed since the mid-90s, and craft beer culture has changed along with it. "Now beers have fans," Sam explains. "They're like rock bands; they have an audience, a fan base, and they have websites where followers show their devotion to certain beers." Sam also sees that people are now flocking to San Diego specifically for the beer — gone are the days when tourism was only based on sunshine, beaches, and Sea World. "The reputation has gone worldwide. It's nuts!"

Reflecting on his role in San Diego's cultural history, Sam appears satisfied. "We've influenced a ton of other bars, which I'm really proud of. Many were customers, like Scot Blair from Hamilton's, who came into Live Wire and said, 'I want to do that, and then some.' We have a neat little group of alumni — people who have a real connection to Live Wire."

MANZANITA BREWING CO.

{TAP FACTS}

- Began pouring:
  2010

- Brewery size:
  3,000 square feet

- Production per year:
  1,200 barrels

- First craft beer
  brewery in the city of
  Santee, California

Manzanita's cofounders, Jeff Trevaskis and Garry Pitman, are working hard to get established in all the right places. They only opened their doors in July 2010, but they have already convinced a lot of the right people that their beer is top quality and their brewery is here to stay.

The owners of one of San Diego's newest breweries met about 12 years ago, when Jeff hired Garry to work at his company. They became friends and soon became brewing buddies. Garry had gotten into homebrewing first, and Jeff decided he couldn't go back to buying mass-produced beer from the store. "So, we started homebrewing together," Jeff recalls.

Cofounders Jeff Trevaskis (left) and Garry Pitman

Garry remembers their first collaboration: "It was a Nut Brown Ale, made from a kit that came from Home Brew Mart. I actually still own the kettle." Jeff says he and Garry spent a few years working on recipes and perfecting their techniques before external circumstances forced a life change. "In December of '09 we both got laid off, and we both decided to take the plunge. We'd been planning it for months — we wanted to get into the brewing business." They had been collecting equipment for a while in anticipation of opening a brewery and pretty much had all the pieces they needed to create a working facility. "It was all in a box in my backyard when we got laid off," Jeff remembers. "We just needed that kick to push us over the edge and get us started."

Manzanita Brewing Co.

SANTEE, SAN DIEGO EAST COUN

A very comfortable tasting room.

They found the perfect space in Santee, where they became the city's first official brewery. Once the brewhouse, kettles, and tanks were set up, Garry and Jeff sprang into production. Garry rattles off the statistics: "For 2010, in seven months of brewing, we produced 195 barrels. For the first quarter of 2011, we did 200 barrels." But Garry is already looking to gear up to full production as soon as possible. "With the equipment we currently have, we can do roughly 1,200 barrels a year," he guesstimates.

Manzanita offers five beer styles as its core lineup: Riverwalk Blonde (Kölsch-style ale), Rustic Horizon Red Ale, Gillespie Brown Ale, a Pale Ale, and an IPA. They are also planning to offer special beers and seasonals once a month or so to start. One of their first specialty beers was called Jazz Man, which was a jasmine-infused Pale Ale. In June 2011, they released their first Double IPA. "We've really worked on creating balanced beers," Jeff explains. "We don't want beers where you drink one and you're done. We've also worked hard on things like how the foam comes down the glass, and how the beer delivers clean flavors."

The past few months have been filled with Jeff and Garry working to open new accounts and finding new markets and customers. Manzanita beers can already be found in more than 60 bars and brewpubs and at more than 120 bottle accounts — and it's all just San Diego so far. "One thing that's shocked us is the growth," Garry says. "We're growing quite fast, just being a small brewery and just producing for San Diego." Jeff adds that they are seeing a lot of locals from Santee supporting the brewery. "There's a lot of local pride associated with us."

Of course, the next step is adding new equipment, expanding production, and looking toward distribution throughout Southern California. It's no surprise that Garry's eyes light up when he talks of some of the things he and Jeff are already discussing, such as going up to a 30-barrel brew system, which would get them as high as 15,000 barrels a year. Of course, even that system may not be big enough for long — not with the pace Garry and Jeff have set so far!

BREWER'S NOTES

RIVERWALK BLONDE ALE: A light, refreshing beer brewed with American barley, American hops, and fermented with Kölsch-style yeast. A welcoming transition beer for those new to craft brews.

RUSTIC HORIZON RED ALE: Delivers a great initial malt flavor with a roasted grain aftertaste and dry Irish finish every time. Great with a cheeseburger.

PALE ALE: A traditional brew. Behind the strong malt and hop flavor rests a fragrant citrus taste followed by a relaxing, dry finish.

GILLESPIE BROWN ALE: A malty and sweet brew followed by a toasted chocolate flavor. Its dark brown appearance and deep roasted aroma translates into a smooth, warm, distinct finish. Pairs well with desserts.

HAVE A BEER WITH THE BREWER:

Sit down with Garry Pitman and a few Manzanita beers:

www.sdtopbrewers.com/manzanita

IPA: Traditional IPA contains a prominent hop aroma and high hop flavor and bitterness. This bright golden brew delivers a sweet flavor with a dry finish. Makes a great marinade.

> FOR MORE BEER INFO, GO TO
WWW.MANZANITABREWING.COM

Chef Ron Oliver: The Marine Room, La Jolla

Chef Ron playfully calls this dish "shrimp-imbap." It is his jazzed-up take on Bibimbap, the classic rice bowl that is a staple of Korean cuisine. One of the main attractions of Bibimbap is the crisp layer of toasted rice that forms on the bottom of the dish. The resulting nuttiness of the rice and the umami flavors of Korean cuisine are a heavenly match for beer, especially the sultry texture and exotic scent of Manzanita's Jazz Man (its jasmine-infused Pale Ale). This recipe is very flexible. You can add or omit vegetables according to the season and your particular region's offerings. Sliced shiitake mushrooms are a great replacement for honshimejis, for example, and you can use cucumber instead of daikon. Just have fun with it.

SHRIMP-IMBAP   Serves 4

Perfect Pairing: Manzanita Jazz Man Pale Ale

FOR THE PICKLED DAIKON:
1 cup daikon radish, peeled and diced
2 teaspoons seasoned rice vinegar
1/4 teaspoon sea salt
1 teaspoon red Korean chile paste
1 teaspoon sesame seeds, toasted

FOR THE SAUCE:
1/4 cup soy sauce
1/4 cup dark brown sugar
1 tablespoon toasted sesame oil
1 large clove garlic, finely grated
1 tablespoon seasoned rice vinegar

FOR THE SHRIMP-IMBAP:
1 medium green zucchini, outer green
   parts only, julienned
1 tablespoon soy sauce
Freshly ground black pepper, to taste
3 cups cooked short-grain brown rice
4 tablespoons toasted sesame oil
12 jumbo shrimp, peeled and
   deveined
1/4 pound spinach leaves, washed and
   stemmed
2 small carrots, peeled and sliced
   1/16-inch thick on a bias
1 small cluster honshimeji mushrooms
Toasted sesame seeds as needed

1. Make the pickled daikon: Combine all the ingredients in a small serving dish. Toss to coat and set aside.
2. Make the sauce: In a small mixing bowl, stir all the ingredients together until the sugar dissolves. Transfer to a serving dish.
3. Make the imbap: In a small bowl, toss the zucchini with the soy sauce and ground black pepper to taste. Set aside.
4. Place the cooked rice in a colander and rinse briefly under cold running water to

remove excess starch. Drain thoroughly and set aside.
5. To a cast-iron skillet over medium heat add 2 tablespoons of sesame oil. Season the shrimp on both sides with freshly ground black pepper. When the oil is hot, sear the shrimp until they are cooked halfway (about 1 minute on each side; less if you are using smaller shrimp). Transfer to a plate.
6. Immediately add the spinach to the skillet. Cook until the spinach is just wilted and transfer to a colander.
7. Drain the zucchini.
8. Rinse the skillet and place it back on medium heat. Add 2 tablespoons of sesame oil. Add the cooked rice to the skillet. Arrange the zucchini, carrots, and mushrooms on top of the rice. Cover the pan with a lid or foil. As the rice cooks in the sesame oil, steam will form. Cook until the carrots are *al dente*.
9. Arrange the spinach and shrimp around the vegetables and replace the lid. Cook until the shrimp are done. Remove the lid and sprinkle with toasted sesame seeds.
10. To serve: Immediately place the pan on a trivet in the center of a dining table. It should still be sizzling. Pour some of the sauce over the dish. Serve remaining sauce and pickled daikon on the side.

After Chef Ron asked culinary student Robin Katz to join the Marine Room's culinary team, he soon discovered Robin's passion for beer and homebrewing. "One of the first things she did was introduce me to the concept of beer floats, and I was immediately fascinated," says Ron. Together, they created a recipe that takes the concept to a new level but is easy to do at home. They added elements that naturally go well with beer — toasty cocoa nibs, nutty macadamias, sour cherries, and caramel in the ice cream. The only way to truly understand the luscious goodness of this wonderful beer float is to try one. Go ahead!

RUSTIC HORIZON BEER FLOAT   Serves 4

½ cup salted macadamia nuts, toasted and
   finely chopped
1 tablespoon real maple syrup or honey
1 pint dulce de leche (caramel) ice cream
¼ cup dried cherries
4 cups Manzanita Rustic Horizon
   Red Ale
¼ cup toasted cocoa nibs

4 large almond biscotti
4 (12-ounce) float-style glass mugs

1. Spread the macadamias evenly on a small plate. Pour the maple syrup onto another small plate. Dip the rim of each mug into the maple syrup, then into the macadamia nuts to form a macadamia rim.

2. Scoop ½ cup of ice cream into each glass. Divide the dried cherries among the glasses.
3. Slowly add 1 cup of Rustic Horizon to each glass. Sprinkle the head of the floats with cocoa nibs.
4. Serve immediately with a biscotti and both a straw and a spoon for maximum enjoyment.

Churros are fun and easy to make at home. Feel free to replace all or some of the spices in this recipe with other seasonings, such as anise, cardamom, or even ginger powder. The most important part of making churros is ensuring that the interior is properly cooked and not pasty. This is achieved by frying them for several minutes as they turn golden brown. The earthy sesame and chocolate flavors along with the spice and subtle saltiness of the seasonings work wonderfully with Manzanita's specialty brew, Pivotal Porter.

SESAME SPICED CHURROS   Makes 8
with Chocolate-Apricot Sauce

Perfect Pairing: Manzanita Pivotal Porter

FOR THE SAUCE:
$1/4$ pound bittersweet dark chocolate, finely chopped
$1/3$ cup sun-dried apricots, thinly sliced
$1/2$ cup half and half

FOR THE BATTER:
1 cup water
1 tablespoon sesame oil
$1/4$ teaspoon salt
1 tablespoon granulated sugar
$1 1/4$ cups all-purpose flour, sifted
2 tablespoons toasted white sesame seeds
2 tablespoons black sesame seeds
Cold water, as needed

FOR THE SEASONING:
$1/2$ cup granulated sugar
$1 1/2$ tablespoons ancho chile powder
1 teaspoon ground cinnamon
1 teaspoon ground star anise
$1/2$ teaspoon sea salt
Corn oil or grapeseed oil for deep frying

1. Make the sauce: In a small bowl, combine the chocolate and apricots and set aside.
2. In a small saucepan on medium heat, bring the half and half to a simmer. Pour the hot cream over the chocolate-apricot mixture and whisk until smooth. Transfer to a serving dish and keep warm.
3. Make the batter: Put the flour in a large

mixing bowl. In a medium saucepan on medium heat, add the water, sesame oil, salt, and 1 tablespoon of the granulated sugar. Bring to a simmer and remove from the heat. Pour the liquid over the flour.
4. Stir the flour mixture vigorously with a wooden spoon to form a dough. Transfer the dough to a mixing bowl.
5. Gently knead the sesame seeds into the dough (it should be very firm but smooth). If it is not smooth, gently knead cold water into it (1 teaspoon at a time) until a smooth dough is achieved. Place the dough into a churrera (churro piping device) or a cloth pastry bag fitted with a medium star tip. Set aside.
6. Make the seasoning: Mix together $1/2$ cup of the granulated sugar, the chile powder, cinnamon, star anise, and salt on a flat plate.
7. In a nonstick sauté pan on medium heat, add the corn or grapeseed oil to a depth of 1 inch. Maintain the oil temperature at 325°F. (If a thermometer is not handy, keep the oil hot but not smoking.) The oil should be hot enough to brown the churros nicely in about 4 minutes, but not faster.
8. Pipe 6-inch-long strips of dough directly into the oil, using a knife to break the dough away from the tip. Fry, turning occasionally until crispy and golden brown, about 4 minutes. Roll churros in the sugar and spice mixture. Serve warm with chocolate-apricot sauce.

MISSION BREWERY

{TAP FACTS}

- Began pouring:
  2008
- Brewery size:
  14,000 square feet
- Production per year:
  Up to 30,000 barrels
- Recent awards:
  More than 15 major
  awards at GABF,
  LA International Beer
  Competition, and
  others.

Dan Selis likes to think big. As the owner and founder of Mission Brewery, he has taken his beermaking operation from the tiny, cramped spaces of his kitchen and garage, to a small pub in La Jolla, to a modest brewery in Chula Vista, and finally to its present location in the historic Wonder Bread Building in downtown San Diego. His newest venue is far from a homemade garage set-up. Mission now occupies more than 14,000 square feet, and has the capacity to produce 10,000-plus barrels a year. The new space also has a gorgeous tasting room that can accommodate up to 400 people.

"I started homebrewing twenty years ago, when I was in college," Dan explains. "Someone showed me how to do my first batch, and I was hooked." He quickly became a homebrew enthusiast and later enrolled in a beer judge certification program (where he shared a classroom with AleSmith's Peter Zien). Dan says that becoming a beer judge "fundamentally changed

Dan Selis

Shiny new tanks fill the brewery's huge brewing area.

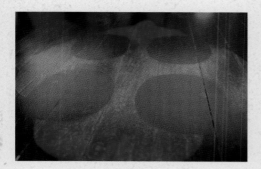

me as a brewer. It took me from an understanding of the process to a level where, when you come out of the training, you can taste a beer and know what happened in the manufacturing to cause a defect or to cause a positive characteristic. When you're judging, you have to not only taste a beer, you also have to give feedback to the brewer."

Most of Dan's brewing career was spent while he was working in a corporate banking job that he loathed. "It sucked. I hated it," he recalls. After 15 years in an office, Dan finally saw an opportunity to get into professional brewing. In 2007, he heard that a brewery that was part of a restaurant in University Town Center (La Jolla), was looking for a brewer or looking to sell its equipment — they weren't quite sure what they were going to do. Dan convinced the owner to let

The new tasting room (right) can accommodate up to 400 people.

him take over the brewery part of the restaurant, and that's where Dan's pro brewing journey began.

Within a year or two, Mission had outgrown its La Jolla space, and Dan moved his operation to Chula Vista, where he also found a way to optimize the resources of a brewery that was underutilizing its equipment. It only took Mission another two years to outgrow the Chula Vista facility, and that growth enabled Dan to make his biggest leap yet. "We entered the beer industry at a great time," he explains. "The industry on its own is increasing double-digits every year. In terms of dollars, it's the hottest sector in alcohol."

Dan attributes a good deal of his success to the quality of his beer and the considerable talents of John Egan, Mission's brewmaster. Up to now, John has focused on brewing five core beers for the brand: three German styles and two IPAs. "We want our beers to be enjoyed by everybody, from beer aficionados to people who may not even typically drink beer." But John clearly has some big plans and new ideas that he's going to explore in the brand new space. "Everything's still a work in progress, especially with the new brewery," he says.

Among its many benefits, the new space will provide lots of new opportunities for Dan and John to get firsthand feedback from all kinds of drinkers. "Up to this point, we haven't been able to sell our beer directly to the public," Dan explains. "Now, we not only get to sell it, we can also use the tasting facility as a lab to create new beers. John will be making a new beer every other month, and we'll test it here, in other bars, and in places outside of San Diego. With that feedback, we can see what's got the potential for production on a larger scale." This "big thought" obviously makes Dan very happy. Smiling, he adds, "I think we have a good shot at becoming a national brand in the next five years."

About the Mission Brewery Name: As a native San Diegan, Dan Selis grew up with an awareness of the Mission Brewery name and a sense that it was a part of the city's rich history. The original Mission Brewery on Hancock Street was founded in 1913 but was shut down during Prohibition. When it came time to name his new brewery, Dan learned that the Mission name was available. "I had a fondness for the name from my childhood, from earlier years where I had always seen the brand 'Mission Brewery' in San Diego." In April 2011, when Mission opened in the historic Wonder Bread Building (built in 1834), the brewery was finally back in downtown San Diego, where it had first begun.

BREWER'S NOTES

MISSION BLONDE: Kölsch-style Ale. Fruitiness complements the blend of Noble hops. Lager-like with its delicate dryness.

MISSION HEFEWEIZEN: Award-winning Bavarian-style Hefeweizen. Hints of banana, clove, and pear all come from an authentic German yeast strain. Bready and unfiltered with a fluffy and creamy texture.

MISSION AMBER: Light and dark with lingering sweet caramel flavor from the use of Caramel, Munich, and Vienna malts. Moderate hop flavor.

MISSION IPA: Big hoppy beer. The hops are complex giving a citrusy, floral, and piney character derived from the use of American hops (Cascade, Centennial, and CTZ).

HAVE A BEER WITH THE BREWER:

Sit down with John Egan and a few Mission beers:

www.sdtopbrewers.com/mission

MISSION SHIPWRECKED DOUBLE IPA: San Diego–style Double IPA. Amazingly balanced and hoppy beer. Smooth finish. Super citrus and grapefruit aromas and flavors.

> FOR MORE BEER INFO, GO TO WWW.MISSIONBREWERY.COM

Executive Chef Karl Prohaska, The Handlery Hotel

Karl Prohaska is a big beer fan. In fact, he's one of the founders of the Mission Valley Craft Beer Festival, which now officially kicks off the San Diego beer festival season in March. Chef Karl recalls that when they hosted the Mission Brewery dinner during Beer Week 2010, he knew he wanted to serve a traditional dish to go with Mission's Blonde Ale. Karl took a classic pairing of light lager beers with sausage and sauerkraut and "dressed it up a bit" — instead of sauerkraut, he pickled mushrooms and carrots and put the Bockwurst on a tartine (a toasted, open-faced sandwich). Says Karl: "Mission's Blonde Ale is such a nice, light, refreshing beer, it marries beautifully with the sour slaw elements. The Bockwurst I used has parsley in it, which brightens up some of the citrus notes, and really helps the beer to shine through. I don't think of my recipe as a 'revision' or 'reinvention' — I think of it more as a 'renovation.'"

BOCKWURST TARTINE   Serves 4 (as an appetizer)

with *Mushroom-Carrot Slaw and Saba-Amber Drizzle*

Perfect Pairing: Mission Brewery Blonde Ale

FOR THE SLAW:
1 pound mushrooms, either shiitake or cremini, thinly sliced
¹/₂ pound carrots, shredded or finely julienned
3 shallots, thinly sliced
2 cups apple cider vinegar
¹/₂ cup light brown sugar, packed
2 tablespoons herbes de Provence
1 lemon, zested

FOR THE DRIZZLE:
2 cups Mission Brewery Amber Ale
2 cups Saba vinegar
   (Saba balsamic vinegar is a specialty balsamic vinegar with a very distinctive, fruit-forward flavor that has a sweetness roughly akin to cane syrup. If Saba isn't available, select a good aged balsamic vinegar.)

FOR THE TARTINE:
4 links bockwurst or weisswurst (such as Schaller & Webber or Ussingers)
1 loaf country bread, unsliced (sourdough, rye, or pumpernickel)

1. Make the slaw: Place the vegetables in a medium bowl. In a small saucepot, mix the apple cider vinegar, brown sugar, and herbes and bring to a boil. Stir frequently to ensure that the brown sugar melts. After the boil, remove the pot from the heat and add the lemon zest. Allow the mixture to cool for 3 minutes before pouring it over the vegetables. Cool slaw completely and reserve.

2. Make the drizzle: In a medium saucepot, mix the beer and Saba vinegar and simmer until it is reduced to about ¹/₂ cup. Reserve.

3. Prepare the tartine: Simmer the bockwurst in hot water. Do not boil. (Bockwurst tend to burst when cooked too aggressively, and that detracts from the overall appearance.) After simmering, the bockwurst may be gently seared in a pan to get some color, if desired. Slice the bread on a bias to create long pieces with diagonally cut sides. Toast the bread and reserve.

4. To serve: Place the sliced toast on a plate and top it with an even layer of slaw. Slice the bockwurst on a bias and shingle it on top of the slaw. Drizzle with the Saba-Amber Ale drizzle and serve with a hearty dollop of whole-grain mustard on the side.

MOTHER EARTH BREW CO.

{TAP FACTS}

- Began pouring: 2010
- Brewery size: 2,500 square feet
- Production per year: 150 barrels
- Homebrew supply shop
- *San Diego Magazine* Best Brewery in North County 2010
- Recent awards: Por Que No? Agave Brown (gold Spirits of SD)

Daniel Love and his son Kamron have made their favorite hobby their new livelihood. After brewing their own recipes for years, these two enthusiasts — along with Daniel's brother Jon — finally opened their own production brewery and homebrew supply shop in May 2010. The dream might never have happened, however, if Dan hadn't met acclaimed San Diego brewer, Lee Chase, at the 2008 Great American Beer Festival in Denver. It was there that Dan asked Lee to be a consultant, to help them figure out how they could be successful in entering the business of professional brewing.

Both Dan and Kamron came straight out of the corporate world — they

Kamron Khannakhjavani (left) and Daniel Love

Colorful signage adorns the tasting room bar.

had lots of homebrew experience, but none on the business end of brewing. "One thing we did know," Dan explains, "is that, if we could brew good beer, we would get the people to come." The hope was that the success of the brewery would help get the name out to the public and would in turn feed the growth of the store.

By the time they were ready to enter the fray, San Diego already had a lot of breweries — and a lot of good ones. So, Dan and Kamron put a good deal of thought into figuring out how to build their own unique identity. "We don't want to compete with anybody — we want to complement," Dan explains. "Our niche is really classic American beer styles, although we do Belgian and German beers, too." Dan also says that being as small as they are affords them a lot of flexibility and leeway in what they brew. "Being a nano-brewery, basically, allows us to change on a monthly basis what we do. A lot of people come in here on a regular basis because they know they're not going to taste the same beer all the time."

Mother Earth offers a number of unique beers that stand out from the pack. Perhaps most notable among them is Por Que No?, which is an American Imperial Brown Ale made with agave syrup. "The syrup is actually unpasteurized from a Tequila distillery in Jalisco, Mexico," Dan explains. "I get the mosto/syrup in a honey form, and it really adds an interesting, earthy taste to the beer. It is added at the end of the boil as another fermentable."

One of Mother Earth's other unique offerings is called Otay, which is an Oatmeal Chocolate Stout. "That's an interesting beer because we don't use the typical grains that you'd use for a stout. I use a lot of Belgian dark malts. It's got a very velvety mouth-feel and is really appealing and delicious." In March 2011, they released The Crucible for the first time — their take on a Black IPA.

Both Dan and Kamron's roots go deep in the homebrew community — they are members of all of the major clubs in the area: Barley Engineers, Barley Literates, and North County Home Brewers. "We count on them, we host their meetings, we're active members, we take part in them. There's a lot of very talented individuals in these clubs. The only thing

they haven't done is stick their toe in the water. They could all do exactly what we're doing here. You don't have to be a rocket scientist to do this, you just have to be willing to risk something."

As a brewer, Dan also thinks it's a great advantage to have a homebrew shop. "On a daily basis, we not only give feedback, but we also get feedback," Dan explains. "And it's an interesting thing because in some places the brewers are behind glass or not accessible. Here, I'm approachable 24/7, and I get a lot of feedback about our beer — whether it's good, bad, or indifferent. Nevertheless, I wholly enjoy it, and it allows me to get better at my craft."

The other element that helps Dan and Kamron

Items from the homebrew shop are part of the tasting room's ambiance.

hone their craft is the sheer level of quality brewing that's going on all around them. "Some of the guys I really look up to as brewers would be Tomme Arthur and Lee Chase. I think both of them are cutting edge; they both know their craft very well. I also really admire Greg Koch at Stone — I think he's really ingenious. And then, there's also Jeff Bagby at Pizza Port Carlsbad, who's been very supportive and a great help to us — the whole company has really helped us get off the ground."

"I think there's still a lot of room for some other breweries in San Diego," Dan explains. "And everybody's growing. There's Iron Fist, right down the road, and Mission Brewing with a huge new place downtown. And we're growing, too. We'll be bottling and increasing our production significantly in the very near future." It's all part, of course, of the homebrewer's dream.

BREWER'S NOTES

PRIMORDIAL IMPERIAL IPA: True to its Imperial roots! This brew clocks in at 9% ABV, and over 100 IBUs! It is made with four varieties of grains resulting in a bold dark amber color and four varieties of hops, creating a subtle citrus aroma, and bitter, hoppy finish.

AULD KNUCKER IPA: A great session IPA. This beer has a balanced mix of three varieties of hops and is dry hopped for a week with Simcoe and Amarillo hops. Can you say grapefruit? If you enjoy the hop characteristics of our DIPA but without that punch-in-the-mouth experience, look no further than Auld Knucker.

SIREN BLONDE ALE: Impossible to have just one. Siren uses Cascade hops and a touch of real honey during fermentation to create a smooth, malty mouthfeel and a crisp carbonating finish.

POR QUE NO? AGAVE BROWN ALE: New collaboration from Mother Earth Brew Co. and El Perdido Tequila. American Imperial Brown Ale is full-bodied, with a subtle, sweet finish, compliments of English crystal malts and pure agave, hand cultivated from the Tequila region of Jalisco, Mexico.

LOS QUATROS AMIGOS SAISON: Second collaboration from Mother Earth Brew Co. and El Perdido Tequila. Belgian farmhouse-style ale is brewed with spices and pure agave, hand cultivated from the Tequila region of Jalisco, Mexico. Its spicy tones and signature Belgian yeast character lend to its incredibly unique flavor.

> FOR MORE BEER INFO, GO TO
WWW.MOTHEREARTHBREWCO.COM

HAVE A BEER WITH THE BREWER:

Sit down with Daniel Love and a few Mother Earth beers:

www.sdtopbrewers.com/motherearth

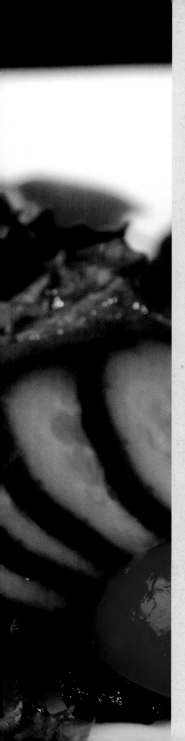

Grant Tondro: URGE Gastropub

When Grant Tondro founded URGE Gastropub with his business partners in 2010, he wanted it to be the first great beer-centric eatery in San Diego's Rancho Bernardo area. To do that, he built in 51 taps (the majority of which are San Diego craft beers), created a menu that incorporates beer in 75 percent of its dishes, and began hosting all kinds of unique special events. "Exceptional quality and selection is our main focus," Grant says. Some customer favorites include a "Deconstructed S'more," made with Double Chocolate Stout, and URGE's signature French fries and house chips, which are all soaked in beer before cooking.

URGE GASTROPUB HERB-AND-HOPS-CRUSTED AHI

with Mixed Greens and Agave-Honey Dressing (created by Jay Mendez, URGE line cook)

Serves 4

Perfect Pairing: Mother Earth's Por Que No? Agave Brown Ale

FOR THE CRUST:
2 teaspoons salt
2 teaspoons freshly ground black pepper
2 teaspoons chili powder
2 teaspoons garlic powder
2 teaspoons fresh oregano, chopped
2 teaspoons fresh basil, chopped
1½ teaspoons crushed hop pellets
  (available at most homebrew supply stores)

FOR THE AHI:
4 (7-ounce) ahi tuna steaks
Olive oil, for brushing

FOR THE AGAVE DRESSING:
2 tablespoons olive oil
2 tablespoons balsamic vinegar
2 cloves fresh garlic, minced
2 tablespoons agave syrup
Salt and pepper to taste

FOR THE SALAD:
4 cups mixed greens
16 slices cucumber
16 cherry tomatoes, sliced
½ cup carrots, shaved

1. Make the crust: Mix all the crust ingredients together in a bowl.
2. Make the ahi: Brush the tuna with olive oil, then coat the tuna with the crust mixture.
3. In a medium pan, heat 2 tablespoons of olive oil until very hot (should be fragrant) and sear the tuna on each side for 90 seconds (2 minutes if you prefer it less red in the center). Remove the tuna from the pan and allow it to cool to warm.
4. Make the dressing: Blend the dressing ingredients in a blender and toss the greens with the dressing. Plate portions of the salad and garnish with cucumber slices, tomatos, and shaved carrots.
5. Slice the tuna, place it on top of the salad, and serve.

NEW ENGLISH BREWING CO.

{TAP FACTS}

- Began pouring: 2008
- Brewery size: 2,000 square feet
- Production per year: 500 barrels
- Recent awards: Brewers Special Brown (silver LACF); Explorer ESB (gold LACF); Troopers Tipple (gold LACF)

Simon Lacey has worked hard to "fit in" with the San Diego beer community. He's not one of the city's "homegrown" brewers; he hasn't formally been part of the beer scene for all that long, and he wasn't originally considered to be "one of the boys" who hung together and drank together in a loose affiliation, talking about beer and trading tips and techniques. But he's gained admission to "the club" — and he's done it through the quality and integrity of the beer that he brews (and by being a super nice guy).

It's not that the other brewers were a particularly tough bunch to break into — in fact, Simon has always been grateful for the true camaraderie and collegiality

Owner-brewer Simon Lacey works the brewhouse as he creates a batch of Explorer ESB.

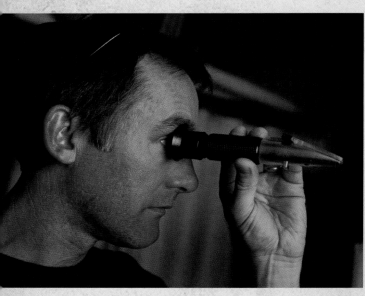

Simon uses his refractometer to check specific gravity (above) and carefully records his numbers in his brew log (below).

he's felt from other San Diego brewers. "One of the main reasons I'm getting out of the corporate world and into beer full-time is because of the camaraderie," Simon explains. He remembers that, back when he first started going to the Brewers Guild meetings, he was struck by the fact that "it was evident that people were all helping each other out. And these were erstwhile competitors, all vying for the same market. And yet, everyone was helping each other out. It was tremendously encouraging and so refreshing — especially after working in the corporate rat race for 20 years."

Originally relocated here from England for his job in high-tech, Simon moved to San Diego in 1995. In 2004, after a layoff, he decided to start a transition to something that was going to be "a little more artisan. Something where I was working for myself." It also seemed to be the right time. "I always loved beer, I knew some guys back in England who owned a brewery, and there were lots of beer-centric things happening in San Diego," Simon explains. So, he went back to England to pick the brains of his brewing buddies, to learn more about the process. "I had been homebrewing at the time, so I had some recipes going. I formulated my ideas for a couple of years, and I interned at a local brewpub to get started. Then I took over another brewpub, worked there for a while, and started New English Brewing Co. in 2007."

Simon's vision for New English was to focus on English styles but with a California twist. "The

Simon puts his West Coast spin on traditional English styles, in part by utilizing a variety of different hops.

company's slogan is 'Traditional New English Style, Authentic West Coast Character.'" What that means, Simon explains, is that he's brewing the typically English-style beers, but he's using some of the nuances and techniques that have been developed in San Diego "to make beers a little more interesting. A little hoppier, for example, but still balanced."

Like all San Diego brewers, Simon does an IPA — but his is different. "Troopers Tipple IPA is really an English-style IPA. It uses English malts and

English hops, as opposed to the West Coast IPAs that are very popular in San Diego with big American hop profiles." The result is also lower ABV (alcohol by volume) than most San Diego IPAs. "I'm a big fan of session beers — beers with very high drinkability," Simon explains. His other core beers include his Why? Not American Wheat Beer, Explorer ESB, and his Brewers Special Brown Ale.

Now, as part of the brewing "establishment," Simon gets constant inspiration from his colleagues. "There are so many great brewers in San Diego," he explains. "Colby Chandler from Ballast Point — he makes such amazing beer. Dan Selis, from Mission Brewery — Dan's a great guy — he's one of the men to watch on the local scene. Chuck Silva, from Green Flash — a great brewer and a fantastic guy. Who wouldn't want to be like that?"

The New English brewery is housed inside the same building that used to be home to the historic Mission Brewery.

BREWER'S NOTES

WHY? NOT AMERICAN WHEAT BEER: Refreshing clean malt flavor and crisp dry finish. Mellow wheat malt body. Filtered. Hand crafted in small batches.

TROOPERS TIPPLE IPA: Thirst-quenching English-style India Pale Ale. Peppery, earthy aroma, medium malt body, balanced bitterness, clean finish.

EXPLORER ESB: Classic English-style ale. Assertively hopped, strong bitter beer, balanced with chewy maltiness, clean, dry, bitter finish. Flavor comes from a blend of caramel and biscuit malts.

BREWERS SPECIAL BROWN ALE: Robust brown ale full of malt character. Complex flavor comes from combination of crystal, victory, and roasted malts.

> FOR MORE BEER INFO, GO TO
WWW.NEWENGLISHBREWING.COM

HAVE A BEER WITH THE BREWER:

Sit down with Simon Lacey and a few New English beers:

www.sdtopbrewers.com/newenglish

**GUNTHER EMATHINGER AND COREY RAPP,
KARL STRAUSS BREWING COMPANY**

For Beer Week each year, participating San Diego chefs get randomly paired with participating breweries for one of the special dinner events of the week. In 2010, Gunther Emathinger, Karl Strauss executive chef, and Corey Rapp, restaurant chef and R&D coordinator, teamed up with New English, which inspired them to create a dish that highlighted Simon Lacey's excellent Brewers Special Brown Ale. In creating this recipe, the chefs wanted to bring out the malt-forward, nutty flavors of the beer while pairing the crisp hop components with a rich, full-flavored meat, such as lamb.

Chefs Emathinger (left) and Rapp

PISTACHIO-CRUSTED LAMB CHOPS Serves 2
with Root Vegetable and Fig Hash and New English Brewers Special Brown Ale au Jus

Perfect Pairing: New English Brewers Special Brown Ale

FOR THE HASH:
1/2 cup dried black mission figs
1 1/4 cups (10 ounces) New English
   Brewers Special Brown Ale
1 medium beet
1/2 cup carrots, peeled, diced into 1/2-inch
   cubes
1/2 cup parsnip root, peeled, diced into
   1/2-inch cubes
1/2 cup yukon gold potatoes, peeled,
   diced into 1/2-inch cubes
1/2 cup sweet potato, peeled, diced into
   1/2-inch cubes
2 tablespoons olive oil
2 tablespoons unsalted butter
1 tablespoon fresh basil, coarsely
   chopped
1 teaspoon fresh rosemary, finely chopped
1 teaspoon fresh sage, finely chopped
Salt and pepper to taste

FOR THE LAMB:
1/2 cup shelled pistachio nuts
1/2 cup panko bread crumbs (or substitute
   plain Italian-style bread crumbs)

1/3 cup unsalted butter
1 (12-ounce) lamb rack, frenched (rib
   ends trimmed)
1 tablespoon olive oil
Salt and pepper to taste

FOR THE JUS:
1 garlic clove, minced
1/4 cup New English Brewers Special
   Brown Ale
1/2 cup veal demi-glace (or substitute
   brown stock, brown gravy, etc.)
1 tablespoon unsalted butter

1. Rehydrate the figs. Remove stems and cut into 1/2-inch dice. Place figs in a small bowl and pour 1/2 cup of Brown Ale over figs. Soak for about an hour.
2. Drain figs and set aside.
3. Begin the hash: In a small pot, cover the beet in cold water and bring to a boil. Cook until tender, approximately 45 minutes. Remove from the water and chill.
4. Preheat the oven to 375°F.
5. In a medium pot, combine the carrots,

parsnips, potatoes, sweet potatoes, and 1/2 cup Brown Ale, cover with cold water, and bring to a boil.
6. Simmer the vegetables for about 15 minutes until tender. Remove from heat, drain, and spread on a baking sheet to cool.
7. Peel the skin from the boiled beet and dice into 1/2-inch cubes.
8. Toss the diced beet with the olive oil, sprinkle with salt and pepper, spread on parchment paper-lined baking sheet, and roast in the oven for 10 minutes, until the edges of the beets turn brown. Remove and chill.
9. Make the crust: In a food processor, pulsate the pistachios and panko bread crumbs until the nuts are medium ground. Add the butter and mix until well incorporated. Set aside.
10. **Prepare the lamb:** Season the rack with salt and pepper.
11. In a large sauté pan, heat the oil to very hot. Add the lamb rack, rounded side facing down, and roast until well browned, about 3 minutes.

12. Bake the lamb in the pan (still round side facing down) in the oven for approximately 5 minutes.

13. Remove the lamb from the oven, turn it round side facing up, and cover the entire surface evenly with the pistachio crust.

14. Return the lamb to the oven and bake for another 4 to 6 minutes for medium rare (internal temperature of 135ºF) or 6 to 8 minutes for medium (internal temperature of 145ºF).

15. Remove the rack from the oven and the pan and place on a serving platter, covered with foil. Let it rest for 3 to 5 minutes.

16. Make the jus: Pour off any oil or grease from the sauté pan and return it to the heat. Add the minced garlic and sauté until lightly browned.

17. Deglaze with the Brown Ale and boil to reduce volume by half. Add the veal demi-glace and bring to a boil.

18. Remove from the heat, whisk in the butter, season with salt and pepper to taste, and set aside.

19. Finish the hash: In a medium sauté pan, heat 2 tablespoons of butter. Add the precooked root vegetables and sauté until the edges of the vegetables turn lightly brown. Add the remaining ¼ cup of Brown Ale and cook until all the beer is absorbed.

20. Add the figs and fresh herbs and sauté for 1 minute.

21. Just before service, add the beets, gently toss and reheat the vegetables, and season with salt and pepper to taste.

22. To serve: Divide the hash between 2 plates, putting each serving in a mound in the center. Cut the lamb rack by slicing between the bones, and place 3 chops on each plate, leaning them against the hash. Pour the sauce over the lamb chops and the hash, and serve immediately.

O'BRIEN'S PUB

LONGTIME CRAFT BEER LOVERS OFTEN REFER TO THE "HOLY TRINITY" OF ORIGINAL SAN DIEGO BEER BARS: Liar's Club, Live Wire, and O'Brien's. These were the businesses that first provided real sales outlets for the area's great brewers. O'Brien's current owner, Tom Nickel, explains: "Back in the mid-'90s and late '90s, there weren't a lot of bars buying San Diego beer, but you could always walk into O'Brien's and find a lot of local taps. There's a lot of history there." Tom also adds that O'Brien's remains a great bar because of its long-standing relationships with brewers. "It means we get a lot of rare beers, a lot of specialty beers, and me being a former professional brewer also certainly helps. I have a very personal relationship with a lot of the breweries we deal with. I'm not just a customer."

Original owner Jim O'Brien opened the pub on January 1, 1994, and became the first account for many of the local breweries in town. Late in 2002, the bar went up for sale, and Tom jumped at the chance. "I'd been a longtime customer and had been a brewer for Oggi's Pizza in Del Mar at the time. It was one of those 'Remington product moments' — you know, 'I liked the company so much I decided to buy it.'" Tom took ownership on January 1, 2003, and has relished every day since. "I'm at the center of my own personal beer playground," he chuckles. "Imagine, if you were five years old and you got to choose all the toys you wanted to play with. That's what I get to do as an adult."

Tom recalls the San Diego scene back in 1995, when he started working at Home Brew Mart, right before Ballast Point opened. It was during that period that the most recent wave of San Diego brewing began to take shape. "Our brewing scene developed differently," Tom explains. "One of the things that helped San Diego stand

Below (left): An O'Brien's burger with onion rings built in; (middle): the pub has long been a craft beer supporter.

out, as the brewing community matured nationally, is that we weren't trying to brew the first Pale Ale, or the first Amber Ale, or the first craft-brewed stout — other breweries like Sierra Nevada, Full Sail, Widmer, they'd already brewed a lot of those beers. So when San Diego matured, we sort of wondered 'what's next?' And so we started doing a lot of barrel-aged beers, double IPAs, stronger beers, and, for whatever reason, double IPAs and the stronger beers sort of 'took' here in town, and they've been our signature ever since."

Early in the evolution of the San Diego brewing scene, there was — according to Tom — a sort of "us versus them" mentality; specifically, San Diego against big national brands that had already established themselves. "The early brewers really banded together," he explains. "We were competing for shelf space with what were already big craft brands, and we weren't really competing with each other — unlike the brewers in

Former pro brewer, Tom Nickel, enjoys a close relationship with many San Diego brewers.

Northern California or Oregon. We were trying to convince people that good beer was being made in San Diego, and I think the early camaraderie of that brewing scene has never been lost. Community spirit is really what sets San Diego apart from a lot of brewing scenes."

So, what's San Diego's biggest problem now? Tom says, "The breweries can't make enough beer. There's too many outlets for it and there's not enough beer being made. I personally hope that we're just at the tip of the iceberg; [that] ten years from now, San Diego beer will be everywhere."

PIZZA PORT BREWING COMPANY

{TAP FACTS}

- Began pouring: 1993

- Brewery size: 4 brewpub locations

- Production per year: 4,500 barrels (4 locations combined)

- Recent awards: Large Brewpub of the Year, Carlsbad (GABF); Small Brewpub of the Year, San Clemente (GABF); 10 GABF and 6 WBC awards in 2010.

If San Diego had an Olympic brewing team, Pizza Port's director of brewpub operations, Jeff Bagby, would be its Michael Phelps. Few other brewers (and their brew teams) have had the consistency and success that Jeff has achieved. At the 2010 World Beer Cup and the 2010 Great American Beer Festival (GABF) alone, Pizza Port's beers claimed a total of 16 medals (10 of San Diego's 16 medals at GABF were Pizza Port's). His Carlsbad team also won Large Brewpub/Large Brewpub Brewer of the Year at the GABF in 2010 (and Pizza Port San Clemente won Small Brewpub/Small Brewpub Brewer of the Year).

One would think that brewers who win so many

Gina Marsaglia founded Pizza Port with her brother, Vince.

awards would be specialists, but that's not the case with Jeff Bagby. "We make a little bit of everything," Jeff says. "You name a style and we've probably done it somewhere along the line." Part of what keeps Jeff going, in fact, is that

he's never locked himself into a rigid lineup. He is basically free to brew whatever moves him at any particular time. "I haven't checked lately, but I'm guessing we make somewhere in the neighborhood of 40 different beers a year here in Carlsbad," Jeff says. "I don't get too crazy with ingredients — I make fairly straight-up beer. But I like to make a lot of different styles. During the past five years, I've collected quite a nice cache of recipes that we've made. Some get made several times a year, some only once a year, some don't even get made once a year. It's  fun for us to continue to experiment and to make new styles." Some of his inspiration comes directly from his fans, who often request their past favorites. "We just got a request to make a Belgian Abbey Dubbel that we haven't made in a few years, so we made it again a week ago," Jeff explains. "The more quirky stuff is also kind of fun because it can be more of a challenge."

No matter what he and his team are brewing, quality and drinkability are always foremost in Jeff's mind. "The thing with Pizza Port, and the things I've tried to instill in the guys that work for me, is making something for everyone, making a wide range of beers, but taking the time and effort to make each

The "Solana," one of Pizza Port's many signature pizzas.

one of those something that they're proud of."

Jeff got the itch to brew while he was still in college. He started his professional career in 1997, brewing for Stone, before moving to Pizza Port Solana Beach in 1999, working on the same team as Tomme Arthur (now of The Lost Abbey). After a stint as head brewer for Oggi's Pizza and Brewing Company in Vista, Jeff came back to Pizza Port in 2005 — this time, the one in Carlsbad, and within months, he was head brewer. He's been there ever since.

Looking toward the future, Jeff would like to get more involved in the homebrew community. He has given a talk to QUAFF, and has recently started a Homebrew Competition at Pizza Port. "We come up with a Best Of Show winner and that homebrewer then works with the Pizza Port brewers and brews their beer at one of the Pizza Port locations," he explains. "It's great to have interaction between pro brewers and homebrewers. A lot of those guys are making amazing beer, too — just on a smaller scale. There's something to be said for that; it's not easy to do. I really admire them."

San Diego's recent international recognition and booming reputation also makes Jeff happy. "I think it's great. You know, there's a lot of guys in town that have been making beer for 10-plus years," he says.

"And I think, for a long time, those breweries have been what we used to say were 'the best breweries no one's ever heard of.' It's kind of funny that all this is snowballing into what it is now, because we've always been saying, 'hey we love this beer and that guy's beer' in town." Jeff also believes San Diego is enjoying the fruits of a whole generation of relatively young and motivated "native" brewers. "There's a large group of guys that grew up in this town and stayed here. Those guys drank the local beers and were turned on to what they tasted. As they began to brew themselves, those local beer flavors fueled the fire that is now the San Diego beer scene."

Darrah Alvarez works the taps at Pizza Port, Carlsbad.

BREWER'S NOTES

CREAM ALE: One of the lightest beers brewed at Pizza Port. Crisp and refreshing.

CALIFORNIA HONEY ALE: Light in color and body. Brewed at all of our locations. Made with the best California honey to produce a subtle aroma and flavor in the finished product.

CHRONIC: Our customers can't get enough of this amber ale that was orginally brewed with hemp seeds but tastes just as good without them.

HOP SUEY DOUBLE IPA: Over 10% of hop insanity! A special treat when it comes around.

HOPS ON RYE BARLEYWINE: The rye shines through on every taste with extreme hoppiness for a barleywine.

NIGHT RIDER IMPERIAL STOUT: Another one of our big beers, coming in at 10%, with a smooth, dark, and rich flavor.

REVELATIONS BELGIAN GOLD: Its light color and body sneaks up on you being 8.5% alcohol by volume.

SHARKBITE RED: Pizza Port's signature brew, made at four locations. Robust red ale made with Centennial and Cascade hops that lend a spicy finish to the beer.

WELCOME BACK WIPEOUT IPA: Our version of the West Coast IPA, coming in at 8.2%. BIG AND HOPPY, huge bitter finish mildly tempered by the large amounts of crystal malt we use. One sip and you'll know why it's called Wipeout.

> FOR MORE BEER INFO, GO TO WWW.PIZZAPORT.COM

HAVE A BEER WITH THE BREWER:

Sit down with Jeff Bagby and a few Pizza Port beers:

www.sdtopbrewers.com/pizzaport

PORT BREWING COMPANY / THE LOST ABBEY

{TAP FACTS}

- Began pouring:
  2006

- Brewery size:
  25,000 square feet

- Production per year:
  12,000 barrels

- Recent awards:
  Red Poppy (bronze
  GABF, silver WBC);
  Hot Rocks Lager
  (bronze GABF, silver
  WBC); Panzer Pilsner
  (silver GABF)

Here's a question: What do you do with a flamethrower and 300 pounds of raisins? Well, if you're Tomme Arthur, you make beer. Tomme is the highly decorated brewmaster and cofounder of The Lost Abbey, along with its sister company, Port Brewing. These two entities are, indeed, very much like a sister and brother — but think Lisa and Bart Simpson. Port Brewing (Lisa) is the straight-laced one; all about great-tasting, classic American and West Coast styles that deliver delicious flavors and the ultimate in drinkability. Lost Abbey (Bart) is the family's "bad boy," where creativity, innovation, and a hint of devilish playfulness are part of every beer they make.

The Port Brewing lineup offers an impressive variety of

Tomme Arthur

The tasting room offers a long list of beers from both Port and Lost Abbey.

styles — from hoppy IPAs and malty reds, to rich, dark lagers and stout-like ales. Hop notes of all strengths take center stage with many of these beers — most notably in the Wipeout IPA, the Mongo Double IPA, and the seasonals such as the Anniversary Strong Ale, High Tide IPA, Hop 15 Ale, and the SPA (Summer Pale Ale).

Most of what Tomme likes to brew for The Lost Abbey has its roots in traditional Belgian styles — but this lineup is not for the faint of heart. Most of

the beers are rich, strong, full-flavored brews that can pack a punch. Tomme likes to utilize ingredients and techniques from all kinds of sources. Some of his beers incorporate fruit elements like raisins, cherries, orange peel, and raspberries. Others use spices, such as ginger, coriander, black pepper, and grains of paradise. He also does a lot with aging in various casks and barrels.

So where do all these ideas come from? "We have three basic sources of inspiration," Tomme explains. "The first are the brewers and people of Belgium. They believe that flavor comes first. When you go to Belgium and drink a beer, there are lots of processes they are using that just don't make sense to the commercial brewers in the rest of the world. But they do it for the flavor, which always comes first to the Belgian people. The second source of inspiration comes from the food world. We look at the culinary arts and ask ourselves, 'what is it about cooking that has applicability in brewing?' A lot of that is balance of flavors, and the expression of flavors. In the case of using raisins, for example, raisins are a fermentable sugar source. It's not uncommon to use fruits in beer, but we take it one step further with our Ten Commandments Ale, and we caramelize the raisins, and that's much like a cooking technique where you're changing the chemical structure of the sugars and changing the flavor." The third major source of inspiration, Tomme says, comes from "friends and the other people we respect and admire as brewers, and we look at the flavors they've achieved. We ask ourselves, 'is there an opportunity to take a piece of what they've done and do something of our own with a similar idea?'"

Part of Tomme's attraction to Belgian styles is the fact that they are, in some ways, less rigidly defined than other styles. "The Belgians don't even typically use the word 'style' much," Tomme says. "They basically just say they brew a brown beer or an amber beer or a blonde beer and it happens to taste this way. And they prize the property of flavor above all else. To them, flavor is the be-all [and] end-all, and how they get there isn't as important as the flavor in the glass."

Like most craft brewers, Tomme is very encouraged by the national trend toward full-flavored beers. "I think we're all very comfortable these days as brewers with the notion that flavor is here to stay.

Whether it's a crisp, clean, hop character that you can't find in a macro-type beer, or an intense maltiness that you can't find in a commercially produced beer, the opportunity for us to be different exists on so many levels."

National trends have, of course, helped to spur the rapid growth of San Diego's craft beer community. Tomme reflects: "I think we're all going to look back and realize that it's not something that happened by mistake. It happened because market conditions were right, there weren't a lot of breweries producing beers in package format, [and] everybody had an opportunity to differentiate themselves. It's still a young culture — you're talking about only a couple of breweries having roots here longer than twenty years. You're looking at  a pretty young community of people. At the same time, a lot of the guys that are making beer here have been doing it for more than ten years, so everybody kind of grew up together, and everyone is happy to support each other. It's just a great place to make beer."

Lost Abbey beers are corked and caged on a modified champagne bottler.

BREWER'S NOTES

THE LOST ABBEY BEERS:

AVANT GARDE: Deep gold in color with hints of biscuits, caramel, and fresh baked bread.

DEVOTION: Light-bodied, refreshingly hoppy blonde, with notes of fresh hay and grassy fields.

INFERNO ALE: Straw yellow, bone dry, and simply labeled "Inferno."

JUDGMENT DAY: A massive, strong, aggressively flavored ale, with notes of dark, roasted, chocolate malts all balanced by the perfect proportions of Challenger and Golding hops.

RED BARN FARMHOUSE ALE: Lightly spiced with organic ginger, orange peels, black pepper and grains of paradise.

LOST AND FOUND: Chef Vince created a special raisin purée for this beer. Malts, raisins, and a fantastic yeast strain working in harmony produce a beer of amazing complexity and depth.

> FOR MORE BEER INFO, GO TO WWW.LOSTABBEY.COM

PORT BREWING BEERS:

MONGO DOUBLE IPA: Hop-forward. Medium to high body. Dry finish with some malted barley sweetness in the finish.

WIPEOUT IPA: Massively hopped India Pale Ale. Only a tidal wave of hops can overcome the surging tide of malt. We invite you to drop in, hang on, and kick out the backside.

SHARK ATTACK: West Coast Double Red Ale brewed with medium crystal malts, Centennial and Cascade hops. Smooth, malty taste with a balanced hoppy finish that includes hints of sweet caramel.

OLD VISCOSITY: Rich, malty blend of newly fermented beer and older, bourbon-barrel-aged beer; dark caramel and chocolate overtones.

> FOR MORE BEER INFO, GO TO WWW.PORTBREWING.COM

HAVE A BEER WITH THE BREWER:

Sit down with Tomme Arthur and a few Lost Abbey beers:

www.sdtopbrewers.com/lostabbey

Vince Marsaglia, Chef on the Loose

Vince Marsaglia has been a key figure in the San Diego beer scene since the '90s, when he opened the first Pizza Port in Solana Beach with his sister Gina. These days, Vince likes to create awesome menus to pair with the many great beers he has available to him. He can often be found catering big events for Port and The Lost Abbey, where he'll roll up with his portable smoker or his specially outfitted trailer and cook up a barbecue or a smoked pig feast for hundreds. When we asked the folks at the brewery for their two favorite Vince recipes of all time, they gave us the two that follow.

POMEGRANATE BONELESS BEER-BRAISED BEEF SHORT RIBS Serves 8

Perfect Pairing: Port Brewing Old Viscosity

FOR THE RIBS:
3 pounds boneless beef short ribs
¼ cup canola oil
4 cups yellow onion (2 cups diced and
 2 cups minced)
2 cups celery, chopped
2 cups carrot, chopped
1 chile pepper (serrano, jalapeño, poblano,
 or your favorite), halved and seeded
4 cloves garlic, crushed
¼ cup balsamic vinegar
1¼ cups pomegranate juice
1¼ cups veal or chicken stock
1 cup Port Brewing Old Viscosity
2 tablespoons unsalted butter
1 tablespoon tomato paste
Salt and pepper to taste

FOR THE GARNISH:
1 cup fresh chives, chopped
1 cup corn kernels, roasted

1. Preheat the oven to 350ºF.
2. Season the ribs with salt and pepper. In a large cast-iron skillet or Dutch oven, heat the canola oil until very hot. Sear the ribs on both sides until brown, remove from skillet, and reserve.
3. To the skillet add the sliced onion, celery, carrots, and chile. Cook until the onions are caramelized. Add the garlic and deglaze the pan with the balsamic vinegar. Add the pomegranate juice and the stock and scrape any brown bits from the side or bottom to dissolve. Add the beer and bring the liquid to a simmer. Add the ribs, submerging them completely, and place the skillet in the oven to bake for 2 to 2½ hours, or until the ribs are fork tender.
4. Remove the ribs from the cooking liquid. Keep warm on a platter. Skim the fat from the liquid and strain liquid into a medium bowl.
5. In a sauté pan, cook the minced onions in the butter until they begin to caramelize. Add the tomato paste and stir for 1 minute. Add the strained cooking liquid and reduce until it thickens enough to coat the back of a spoon.
6. To serve: Cut the ribs into portions and coat them in sauce. Garnish with chives and roasted corn kernels. Also great with roasted black pepper fingerling potatoes.

VINCE'S LOST ABBEY STEAMED MUSSELS   Serves 8

Perfect Pairing: Lost Abbey Devotion

4 pounds fresh mussels
1 medium tomato, finely diced
1 cup green bell pepper, finely diced
1 cup red onion, finely diced
1 chile pepper of your choice (serrano, jalapeño, red fresnos, or your favorite), finely minced
2 cloves garlic, chopped
4 tablespoons unsalted butter
2 tablespoons Cajun spice blend
2 cups Gueuze (Belgian Lambic-style beer)
1 cup chardonnay (a non-oaky one)
1 lemon, zested and juiced
1½ cups fresh cilantro or parsley, chopped
Salt and pepper to taste

1. Thoroughly wash and debeard the mussels. Keep them cold while you work, and discard any mussels that will not stay closed (even after you run them under cold water).
2. In a very large sauté pan, sauté the tomatoes, peppers, onions, chile, and garlic in 2 tablespoons of the butter until the onions are translucent. Add the Cajun spice and stir.
3. Add the mussels, beer, and chardonnay. Stir to mix. Cover and simmer for 5 minutes.
4. Check the mussels and remove them just as they open. (Mussels all cook at different rates, so removing them just as they open prevents overcooking.) Discard any mussels that do not open fully. Set aside in a serving bowl.
5. Add the remaining butter, lemon zest, and juice to the cooking liquid and reduce slightly. Stir in the chopped cilantro or parsley.
Pour the sauce over the mussels and serve immediately with your favorite crusty bread.

PUBCAKES

Above: Misty Birchall turned a unique hobby into a full-time business. Right: A fresh batch of Cup O' Hefen.

BEER IS GOOD. CUPCAKES ARE GOOD. BUT BEER IN CUPCAKES? THAT'S GREAT! And that's the concept behind PubCakes, one of San Diego's newest and most innovative bakery businesses.

PubCakes founder Misty Birchall "sort of" came up with the concept of beer cupcakes by accident. When she got out of the navy (where she was a linguist and spoke fluent Farsi), Misty worked in an office where she was in charge of making the cakes. One of her good friends and office mates was really into beer, and the two of them began to frequent many of San Diego's hottest beer locales. "We'd go to Toronado a lot, in North Park," she recalls. When it came time for Misty to make a birthday cake for her friend, she wanted to do something with beer. "I found this Guinness Chocolate Cake recipe," she remembers, "and I thought, let's take this one step further and make it an Irish Car Bomb (the drink with the Bailey's and Jameson) [cake]. So I filled it with Bailey's buttercream frosting and topped it with a Jameson's whiskey chocolate ganache. It was good! REALLY good!"

With the batter she had left over from that first cake, Misty made cupcakes and brought them to her friends at Toronado. And, at that point — as she relays it — she became obsessed. "I wondered if I could find other recipes with beer in them. But I couldn't." So she began making up recipes of her own.

The second kind of cupcake she made was the Cup o' Hefen, which is made with Ballast Point Wahoo Wheat Beer. When she brought those to her friends at Toronado, she knew she was on to something. "I almost cried when they asked me to start making them for the bar," Misty says.

Soon, Misty was spending all her free time researching other recipes, baking, and developing new ideas. At one point, someone who tasted one of her creations told her it was the "best cupcake he'd ever had." That same person asked Misty why she wasn't in business, which finally got her thinking about doing the beer and cupcake thing seriously and on a larger scale.

Needless to say, at first, funding was a struggle. "I contacted my parents and my friends and asked for donations. My aunt and uncle gave me money, too." And that's how it started. Misty baked for a number of local businesses — delivery only — and did most of her production in a rented kitchen space, working from 10 p.m. to 4 a.m. each day. Eventually, she got a grant through a navy program that helps to fund retired members who have a disability (Misty's was carpal tunnel syndrome). With that, she expanded her business and got a real commercial kitchen space, which also provides a retail outlet.

Now, Misty spends a great deal of her time trying new beers and devising new recipes. She's particularly proud of "Red Velvet Glove" made with Iron Fist Brewing Co.'s stout called Velvet Glove. She also opted to make a more traditional milk-based frosting, in which the milk was steeped with star anise, and combined with a reduction of the Velvet Glove. "It's a play on the traditional red velvet cake, but with a PubCakes flair," Misty says, smiling.

PubCakes can now be found in more than half a dozen San Diego locations, including KnB Wine Cellars, Toronado San Diego, and the UCSD Coffee Cart. They can also be purchased retail at the PubCakes store on El Cajon Boulevard in La Mesa.

This was one of Misty Birchall's earliest beer creations. Enjoy!

CUP O'HEFEN CUPCAKES WITH CITRUS BUTTERCREAM   Makes 24

Perfect Pairing: Ballast Point Wahoo Wheat

BATTER WET INGREDIENTS:
- 1 (22-ounce) bottle Ballast Point Wahoo Wheat
- 3 cups unsalted butter (1 cup softened)
- 2 tablespoons honey
- 2 eggs

BATTER DRY INGREDIENTS:
- 3 cups self-rising cake flour
- 2 teaspoons baking powder
- 1 teaspoon baking soda
- 2 teaspoons ground cloves
- 4 teaspoons ground coriander
- 2 cups golden brown sugar, packed

FOR THE BUTTERCREAM:
- 1 cup unsalted butter, softened
- 1 lemon, zested and juiced
- 2 oranges, zested and juiced
- /4 teaspoon salt
- 4 cups powdered sugar, sifted
- 2 tablespoons lemon juice (from zested lemon)
- 2 tablespoons orange juice (from zested orange)

1. Preheat the oven to 350°F.
2. **Prepare the batter:** In a medium saucepot, bring the beer to a boil, lower the heat to a simmer, and reduce by a third, to 2 cups. Add 2 cups of the butter and the honey.

Continue heating until butter is melted. Set aside and allow to cool to room temperature. (Note: if the butter cools for too long, it will solidify and need to be melted again.)
3. While the beer mixture is cooling, place 24 cupcake liners into a muffin pan.
4. In a separate bowl, sift together the dry ingredients, except the brown sugar. Set aside. In a large mixing bowl, cream the remaining 1 cup of softened butter and the brown sugar on the highest mixer setting. You will know when creaming is complete when the butter and sugar lighten

and also become about a third larger in size. Add the eggs and beat well. Set the mixer to low and slowly add the beer mixture. Finally, slowly add the dry ingredients.
5. Using an ice cream scooper (or a large spoon) fill the cupcake liners about three-quarters full. Bake for about 15 minutes, rotating the pan in the oven half way through the cooking time for even baking. The cupcakes are done when a knife or toothpick inserted into the center comes out clean. Remove the cupcakes from the pan as soon as they have cooled enough to touch, or else you risk steaming the bottoms.
6. **Make the buttercream:** In a mixing bowl fitted with a whisk attachment, mix the butter, zests, and salt on high until well combined. Add the powdered sugar and mix on low speed until well blended, and then increase the speed to medium and beat for another 3 minutes. Add the juices and continue to beat on medium speed for 1 minute more, adding more orange juice if needed for spreading consistency.
7. Fill a piping bag with a #9 round decorating tip to get the same look achieved by PubCakes. Sprinkle with ground coriander.

QUAFF HOMEBREWERS

ASK ANY PRO BREWER IN SAN DIEGO WHERE HIS OR HER PASSION FOR BEER ORIGINATED, and chances are they will answer "from homebrewing." Ask those same brewers what keeps the San Diego beer scene so vibrant, and chances are they will answer, "It's our connection to the homebrew community."

San Diego has had an active homebrew community for many years. QUAFF (Quality Ale and Fermentation Fraternity) goes back to the late 1980s, when it was founded by Audrey and Owen Eckblum, who owned a homebrew shop in El Cajon. Longtime member and past president Dion Hollenbeck remembers that even from its earliest days "the instructional, educational mentality of QUAFF was very, very good."

The group started out initially as a social organization but soon evolved into a beer evaluation forum and an educational endeavor. By 1995, with

Beer judge Jim Crute (center) confers with QUAFF senior member (and award-winning homebrewer) Paul Sangster during the 2011 competition.

roughly 40 members, the group offered its first Beer Judge Certification Program but found that it didn't have enough "experts" to teach prospective students. Dion recalls that "instead, we required each student to pick a particular beer style, to research it, and to present it to the group. What we found was, when you research and present a topic to other people, you know it."

Many people credit the growth of the homebrew community for fueling the innovation and quality that comes out of San Diego, the city that has become known as "the Napa Valley of Beer." Harold Gulbrandson, senior member of QUAFF and past president, says, "Many of the homebrewers who have never gone pro continue to challenge pro brewers to experiment with different styles, to make changes, to push the envelope." Many homebrewers have also brewed in collaboration with professional breweries — Sculpin IPA, for example, began as a homebrew and was ultimately the end result of homebrewers collaborating with Ballast Point's Specialty Brewer,

Colby Chandler. Dion adds that pro brewers need homebrewers because "they're the most educated users that [pro brewers] have. Certainly the homebrewers are not going to hold back. We're gonna tell them exactly what we think of their beers. We are a benchmark of whether they are doing well or not — regardless of sales. We're the people who really care how good that beer is."

San Diego's pro brewers support the homebrew community in many ways as well. "It's clearly a two-way street," Harold says. "The support that the homebrewers get from the pro brewers in San Diego [is] a relationship don't see in a lot of other places around the country. I think we have a kind of unusual environment here that's really unique."

Each year, QUAFF holds a homebrew competition, where pro and amateur brewers judge the best beers in 23 different categories. In 2011, there was a record number of entries (501), and QUAFF decided to create two new categories by giving two of the most popular styles their own category: American Pale Ale and American IPA. Highly decorated homebrewer Paul Sangster, who organizes the competition, explains that "there was a lot of buzz in 2011 because of the big news that San Diego was going to host the National Homebrewers Conference. So, there was a lot of interest from all over the country, and all the local clubs are really geared up for the championships."

Homebrews await evaluation at the 2011 QUAFF competition.

ROCK BOTTOM GASLAMP

{TAP FACTS}

- Began pouring: 1998
- Brewery size: 1,000 square feet
- Production per year: 1,000 barrels
- 9 core beers
- Only craft brewery in the Gaslamp
- Restaurant features beer-friendly food

Jason Stockberger is the brewmaster at the downtown San Diego location, located smack dab in the middle of the city's popular Gaslamp District. Over the years, Jason has developed his lineup of beers — mostly his take on classic American, German, and English styles — and has brought his unique charm and enthusiasm for brewing to the downtown scene.

Jason became a brewer "the old-fashioned way," he apprenticed with a master. He learned his craft from one of the best: "Johnny O" (John Oliphant), who is well-known in San Diego brewing circles. As Jason says, "Johnny O taught me everything I know about beer." After working with Johnny O for about six years, it was time for Jason to take the helm.

Today, Jason is brewing up about 1,000 barrels a year (roughly 2,000 kegs) and selling it all right there at the brewery-restaurant. Though patrons can purchase the beer in growlers, there's no bottling and no distribution off the premises. "We like the fact that you have to come into the restaurant to get these handcrafted beers that you can't find anywhere else," Jason says, "and every Rock Bottom makes different beers."

There are a total of nine styles regularly on tap at Rock Bottom Gaslamp, with another two or three that are rotated seasonally. Rock Bottom's brewers all like the fact that the "corporate office" gives each location the freedom to brew

Jason Stockberger works his mash tun the old-fashioned way.

their own collection of recipes, though there is some overall supervision by a regional brewmaster who works with all the locations to ensure a certain level of quality and consistency. Jason has worked in partnership with La Jolla brewmaster Marty Mendiola to construct recipes that fit the specific demographic of the downtown location. "Every area is different," Jason explains. "Not everybody likes the same kinds of beers. People in different areas like different kinds of beers." Jason has noticed a recent surge in the popularity of Kölsch-style ales and wheat beers, such as Rock Bottom's Belgian White Wheat Ale. "I used to only make it once a year," Jason explains, "but now I keep it on all year round because people are asking for it all the time. Especially when the weather turns warmer."

Jason's personal favorites include Rock Bottom Red Ale, which has toasted malts and a caramel kind of flavor. "A real nice body, and a real nice hoppiness — it's probably my most balanced beer, with malt and hops. This is the beer that started me loving Rock Bottom beers, so it will always be one of my favorite beers here." His favorite IPA? Hop Bomb: A specialty beer that is light in color, hopped three times in the kettle and once with a heavy dry hop into the fermenter. "It's got a lighter malt profile," Jason explains, "and a really aromatic hoppy quality from the Columbus and Centennial hops, real high Alpha hops." Jason's absolute favorite beer of all is his Sunset Stout. "It's silky and smooth, with a wonderful head, and a small, fine nitro bubble. It's got so much going on — roasted flavors, chocolate, coffee, and sweet toffee."

There are still a bunch of new beers that Jason has on his list to try his hand at. At the top of the list would be the smoked beers; specifically, a smoked porter. "I'd love to do some beers where I can bring out those smoky, musty flavors." His other goal is to do a Dunkelweizen, which, he says, is "probably one of the simpler styles of beer to make, but I haven't done that yet."

Lots of brewpubs keep their tanks, equipment, and brewers behind glass all the time, but at Rock Bottom Gaslamp, Jason is always eager to come out and greet his public to talk beer. His love for what he does is infectious, and the pride he takes in the beers he makes is inspiring. That's why Jason truly deserves to be called one of San Diego's "top brewers."

BREWER'S NOTES

ROCK BOTTOM KÖLSCH ALE: Traditional German-style ale, light, crisp, and refreshing.

ROCK BOTTOM IPA: Classic, golden-hued ale is brewed with the finest hand-selected hops from the Pacific Northwest for an assertive, citrus-hop flavor.

ROCK BOTTOM RED ALE: Flavorful and complex, our Red Ale is copper in color and medium-bodied with a rich malt profile. Crystal hops lend a robust, fruity hop character for balance.

ROCK BOTTOM BROWN ALE: Traditional English-style brown ale that is dry and has a subtle blend of roasted grains.

ROCK BOTTOM SUNSET IMPERIAL STOUT: Nitrogenated stout is rich, creamy, and has flavorful notes of chocolate, coffee, and toffee.

ROCK BOTTOM BELGIAN WHITE WHEAT ALE: Pale with a touch of haze. Gets its unique phenolic flavor from orange peel, coriander, and Belgian yeast.

> FOR MORE BEER INFO, GO TO WWW.ROCKBOTTOM.COM

HAVE A BEER WITH THE BREWER:

Sit down with Jason Stockberger and a few Rock Bottom beers:

www.sdtopbrewers.com/
rockbottomgaslamp

ROCK BOTTOM LA JOLLA

{TAP FACTS}

- Began pouring: 1998
- Brewery size: 1,000 square feet
- Production per year: 1,000 barrels
- 9 core beers
- Recent awards: Rudolph's Red (gold WBC); Longboard Brown (silver WBC); Ragtop Red (bronze WBC, bronze GABF); Moonlight Porter (silver GABF)

Rock Bottom La Jolla brewmaster Marty Mendiola wants everyone to know that even though Rock Bottom is a chain, every location has its own brewer who brews his or her own unique recipes. Marty's brewing record is a perfect testament to that: At the 2010 World Beer Cup, his beers won three medals, including a gold. "The great thing about Rock Bottom," Marty explains, "is that they kind of let us run the breweries independently. So, I've been able to do all kinds of recipes — with IPAs alone, I've probably brewed 30 to 40 different recipes over the years."

It all began for Marty with a love for homebrewing. "I bought my first kit back in 1993 at the Home Brew Mart in Linda Vista," Marty recalls. "I made an Amber Ale. I just loved it. I remember the first batch: I bottled it, put it in the fridge, then popped it open, and it was actually good!" With

Brewmaster Marty Mendiola

his newfound bug for brewing, he went to UC Davis in 1997 to enter the master brewer's program. From UC Davis, Marty went out to Rock Bottom in Colorado

Seasonal and specialty beers fill out the core lineup at Rock Bottom La Jolla.

to work as an assistant for a couple of years and to learn the "real life" lessons of brewing in a real brewery setting. As a longtime San Diegan, Marty jumped at the opportunity when the La Jolla location's brewmaster position became available in 1999 — and he's been there ever since. "Brewing in San Diego has made me a better brewer," Marty explains. "The camaraderie and competition that we have here plays a big role."

The La Jolla location is a high-profile and very busy place to create beer. Speaking of his basic lineup, Marty says, "We're definitely more of an 'ale' brewery. We're quite busy at this location and have limited tanks and space, so it would be difficult to do a whole lot of lagers, which need a little bit more time. My bread and butter has been the ales — Irish Red, English Brown, and the IPAs, which are so popular — especially here in

San Diego. It's hard to keep up." Marty likes to keep his hand in a bunch of styles, including the Belgians, such as Dubbels or his Abbey Ale, which have "a lot of fruity things going on." He notes that he's "swayed a number of wine drinkers with Belgian styles" and finds that a lot of wine drinkers (and a lot of women drinkers) seem to embrace the qualities of Belgian styles more readily than others.

Reflecting on his recent successes in competitions, Marty goes back to crediting the San Diego brewing culture for supporting him and keeping him on track. "We have this great thing: We're competitors, but we're also compatriots. If you go to the [Brewers Guild] meetings you can ask 'how'd you do this?' and they may not give you every last detail, but you'd be surprised at how helpful they will be. It's really helped my beers over the years." He adds, "Also Rock Bottom's having the confidence in us, letting us brew our own recipes, that's really been invaluable."

BREWER'S NOTES

RAGTOP RED ALE: A traditional Irish red, medium-bodied, with soft, caramel maltiness. Well balanced with a nice addition of hops, but not overly hoppy.

RUDLOPH'S RED: Gold medal winner. American-style red ale with hop flavor and aroma like an IPA, with the addition of crystal malts to give it a deep red color and a rich caramel malt flavor.

LONGBOARD BROWN ALE: English-style brown, cocoa nuttiness; soft, dark maltiness; creamy texture, with hops in the background.

OATMEAL STOUT: Rich-bodied, with a full, creamy head. Toasted oatmeal and roasted coffee aromas mix with dark chocolate, vanilla, nutty, and malty flavors in the mouth.

NORTH STAR IPA: San Diego West Coast–style IPA. Very hoppy, fresh hop aromas of citrus and pine, with a medium mellow bitterness on the tongue.

FALLEN ANGEL BELGIAN STYLE GOLDEN ALE: Belgian-inspired golden ale is a pale golden color with a smooth, rich, malt character. Special Belgian yeast and a warmer fermentation give this ale a complex, fruity flavor and aroma.

> FOR MORE BEER INFO, GO TO WWW.ROCKBOTTOM.COM

HAVE A BEER WITH THE BREWER:

Sit down with Marty Mendiola and a few Rock Bottom beers:

www.sdtopbrewers.com/ rockbottomlajolla

Executive Chef Alberto Lucatero, Rock Bottom La Jolla
Rock Bottom La Jolla is a happening place, and Chef Alberto Lucatero is frequently preparing a menu for some upcoming special beer dinner or event. With the great variety and quality of the beers being brewed by Marty Mendiola and assistant brewer Russell Clements, Alberto is finding constant sources of inspiration. For a Beer & Chocolate Dinner he recently hosted, Alberto incorporated cocoa or chocolate into every dish — and paired each dish with a special Rock Bottom beer. The recipe that follows is from that beer dinner.

SEARED PORK TENDERLOIN   Serves 4 to 6

Perfect Pairing: Naughty Scot Scottish Ale

FOR THE PORK:
8 cups Rock Bottom Great White Lager
2 Granny Smith apples, peeled, cored, and cut into quarters
3 cloves garlic, minced
2 pounds pork tenderloin, trimmed of excess fat
3 tablespoons olive oil

FOR THE CRUST:
3 tablespoons cocoa nibs
1 tablespoon chile pepper flakes
1 tablespoon ground cumin
2 teaspoons ground mustard seed
2 teaspoons allspice
3 tablespoons brown sugar
2 tablespoons kosher salt
1 teaspoon cinnamon
1 teaspoon ground coriander

FOR THE DEMI-GLACE:
1 cup dry red wine
1 cup Rock Bottom Great White Lager
1 teaspoon fresh rosemary, minced
1 jar (8 ounces) chicken demi-glace
    (available locally and through online gourmet retailers)
1 tablespoon cocoa powder
1 tablespoon brown sugar

1. Make the pork marinade: In a blender, purée the beer, apples, and garlic until smooth. Place the pork in a dish, cover with the marinade (make sure the pork is completely submerged), and refrigerate for 24 hours.

2. Preheat the oven to 350°F.

3. Make the crust: In a medium mixing bowl, combine all the ingredients with a whisk.

4. Cook the pork: Remove the pork from the marinade and roll it in the crusting mix (make sure that all sides are well coated). In an oven-proof skillet, heat the olive oil until very hot (almost smoking). Sear all sides of the pork (about 40 to 50 seconds per side), and bake for 35 to 40 minutes, or until the internal temperature reads 145°F to 155°F.

5. Make the demi-glace: In a medium saucepot, combine the red wine, the lager, and the rosemary leaves, and boil until reduced by half. Strain the liquid to remove the rosemary, and return the liquid to the pot. Add the demi-glace, cocoa powder, and brown sugar to the mixture and bring the liquid back to a simmer. Turn heat to low.

6. Remove the pork from the oven and allow it to rest for 10 minutes before slicing.

7. To serve: Fan out slices of pork on each plate alongside a flavorful starch — such as sweet potatoes, garlic mashed potatoes, or celery root purée — and drizzle the demi-glace over the meat.

STOUT ONION SOUP

Serves 8 to 10

Perfect Pairing: Rock Bottom Stout

¼ cup olive oil
16 cups sliced onions (brown or yellow)
16 cups low-sodium beef broth
1 medium bulb garlic, minced
2 bay leaves
8 to 10 sprigs fresh thyme
1 cup cream sherry
2 cups Rock Bottom Stout
4 tablespoons chicken demi-glace *(available locally and through online gourmet retailers)*
1 French baguette, sliced
3 tablespoons unsalted butter
2 cups grated Gruyère cheese, for topping

1. In a large stockpot, heat the oilve oil on medium-high heat. Add the onions and sauté until they are golden brown (about 20 to 30 minutes).
2. Use about 1 cup of the beef broth to deglaze the bottom and sides of the pot, and add the garlic. Stir well.
3. Add the remaining beef broth, the bay leaves, and the thyme.
4. Add the sherry and stout, and cook until the liquid is reduced by about one-third. Add pepper and taste. Adjust seasoning if necessary.
5. Put the baguette slices under a broiler to toast. As soon as they are brown, remove and butter them.
6. To serve: Place one slice of baguette in each oven-proof bowl and ladle in soup to fill. Cover the tops with a generous layer of Gruyère. Place the bowls under the broiler (watching closely) until the cheese bubbles and starts to brown slightly. Remove and serve immediately with more crusty bread.

STONE BREWING CO.

- Began pouring: 1996
- Brewery size: 55,000 square feet
- Production per year: More than 100,000 barrels
- Stone IPA: World's longest full-time brewed West Coast IPA
- Recent awards: Stone Smoked Porter with Chipotle (silver GABF); Stone Sublimely Self-Righteous Ale (bronze GABF)

One of the first things that strikes you when you visit Stone Brewing Co. is that the place looks incredible. The large brewery sits alongside a huge, high-ceilinged bistro restaurant that overlooks a beautiful one-acre beer garden. The view to the outside is courtesy of 20-foot floor-to-ceiling glass panels that do a great job of bringing the San Diego sunshine indoors.

And there's stone everywhere. Stone fire pits, stone walls, stone accents. There's even a huge stone (most would call it a boulder) sitting in the entranceway to the bistro.

Cofounders Greg Koch (left) and Steve Wagner

The impeccable design of the place, along with the wonderful space it creates for enjoying all kinds of beer, is a testament to one of San Diego's biggest beer success stories. Of course, Stone didn't start out this way. Like most businesses, it had much humbler beginnings.

Stone cofounders Greg Koch and Steve Wagner first met each other through music. In 1989, Greg opened Downtown Rehearsal music studios in Los Angeles, and Steve's band was one of Greg's first tenants. A few years later, completely by coincidence, Steve and Greg spotted each other at a UC Davis beer class called "A Sensory Evaluation of Beer." It was during this class that the two realized they had compatible palates and shared a passion for the same kinds of beer.

Their first brewing collaborations took place in Steve's Los Angeles kitchen

around 1992. As Greg remembers it, "I was basically the homebrew lackey — Steve had quite a bit of brewing experience and knowledge. So, naturally, I fell into the number-two position." Steve and Greg fondly recall their early days, experimenting with recipes and techniques. The first beer they brewed was an Altbier. At one point, early on, they tried to do a date fruit beer. "That was a miserable failure, unfortunately," Greg says.

It was Steve's extensive homebrewing experience and Greg's successful background in business that eventually convinced them to become a team. They

found investors, quit their day jobs, and opened Stone Brewing Co. on February 1, 1996, in San Marcos, California. By July 26, the brewery was officially open for business, and the first Stone beer was tapped.

Greg and Steve were always convinced that their brewery could be successful, even though they didn't want to make "mainstream" products. Their vision was to brew full-flavored beers with strong character and distinctive personalities. "We were determined to do our thing, and do it differently — to be unique," Greg remembers, "and in doing that, I think we showed everyone that you can still be successful." Part of their success came through constant innovation — playing with flavors and ingredients. One of their creations, Arrogant Bastard Ale, was arguably the very first American Strong Ale. It created a whole new category for craft beer.

As brewmaster, Steve originated all of Stone's first recipes and created them with a unique vision in mind. Steve continues to be an integral part of recipe creations today, though he notes that now it's much more of "a collaborative process."

Bottles whiz by on Stone's state-of-the-art bottling line.

Stone Brewing World Bistro & Gardens, which offers an extensive menu and more than 100 beers from around the world, is the largest restaurant buyer of local organic produce in San Diego.

Head brewer Mitch Steele explains that his goal "is to make Steve's recipes come out consistently on the large scale. We've also had to put some structure into the beers we make on this system to make sure the beers taste great all the time." Mitch adds that he works hard to maintain the classic Stone "identity," which he calls "big flavor." He goes on to explain, "It's not necessarily high alcohol, or high amounts of hops or bitterness, just an intense flavor."

Greg and Steve's dedication to their vision paid off. Stone's production volume has steadily increased every year since the company's founding in 1996,

when they produced a little over 400 barrels. Today, the company exceeds 100,000 barrels per year, and there's no end in sight.

In fact, the company is almost growing too fast for Greg and Steve to keep up. In 2009, production volume increased by nearly 25 percent. Stone beers are now distributed in 36 states (plus Washington, DC) and have enjoyed modest distribution in Japan, England, and Sweden. And what's on the horizon? Well, Greg and Steve say that plans are well under way to open a brewery in Europe. If and when they do, they would be the first American craft brewers ever to do so.

Meanwhile, there are plenty of milestones being established here at home. Stone has been one of San Diego's fastest-growing companies for many years and is one of the county's most active beer-education hubs. And the beers continue to reach more and more people every day. Greg is happy to point out that "Stone IPA is now the longest full-time brewed West Coast IPA on the planet, and Stone Ruination IPA was the first full-time brewed and bottled double IPA on the planet."

BREWER'S NOTES

STONE PALE ALE: Robust, smooth, and full-flavored. A delicate hop aroma is complemented by a rich crystal maltiness.

STONE SMOKED PORTER: Dark, smooth, and complex, with rich chocolate and coffee flavors balanced by a subtle smokiness, this brew is equally delicious with meats or fine chocolates.

STONE IPA: Huge hop aroma, flavor, and bitterness throughout. Medium malt character with a heavy dose of Centennial hops.

STONE LEVITATION ALE: Rich malt flavors, a big hoppy character, citrus overtones (courtesy of the hops and our special brewers yeast) and modest alcohol.

STONE RUINATION IPA: Massive hop monster has a wonderfully delicious and intensely bitter flavor on a refreshing malt base.

STONE CALI-BELGIQUE IPA: A California-style IPA, with an undeniable Belgian influence. A carefully selected Belgian yeast strain illuminates a fascinating new aspect of what is otherwise quite simply Stone IPA.

STONE SUBLIMELY SELF-RIGHTEOUS ALE: A Black IPA, first brewed in 2007 as the Stone 11th Anniversary Ale. A perfect balance of black maltiness and roastiness with big IPA-style hoppiness. Medium-bodied, rich, but easy to drink.

ARROGANT BASTARD ALE / OAKED ARROGANT BASTARD ALE / DOUBLE BASTARD ALE
These are aggressive (strong) ales. Full-flavored, hoppy, and wildly aromatic. You probably won't like them. It is quite doubtful that you have the taste or sophistication to be able to appreciate ales of this quality and depth.

► FOR MORE BEER INFO, GO TO WWW.STONEBREW.COM

HAVE A BEER WITH THE BREWER:

Sit down with Mitch Steele and a few Stone beers:

www.sdtopbrewers.com/stone

Executive Chef Alex Carballo: Stone Brewing World Bistro & Gardens

Some chefs have huge wine cellars from which to draw inspiration, others live in the Tuscan countryside or on an island in the Caribbean. Chef Alex Carballo has a garden on the property — as well as access to Stone Farms — but he also has a world of beer at his fingertips every day. "We have almost 100 bottles on our list here," he says with a smile. "No matter what I feel like doing, I know I can find something to pair with it." At Stone Brewing World Bistro & Gardens, Alex is all about creating unique, beer-friendly food that highlights the many wonderful flavor components of beer. "The maltiness of some beers, the flowery hoppiness or spiciness of other beers, the smokiness of a smoked porter — these are all flavors that blend extremely well with food." Alex uses some basic guidelines for creating beer recipes. "Cooking with beer can be difficult if you're not using beers with a relatively high sugar content, such as a porter or a stout. These beers will caramelize and reduce, and blend in nicely with all sorts of dishes. When you get into the ales, such as the IPAs and the double IPAs, those are what I call the 'quick-fire' beers. You don't want to cook them too much or you get a secondary bitterness in the food — the same bitterness you get on your palate when you drink them."

STONE BISTRO SALAD WITH HOPS VINAIGRETTE
Serves 4

Perfect Pairing: Stone IPA

FOR THE VINAIGRETTE:
Yields 4 cups
³/₄ cup roasted garlic, whole cloves
³/₈ cup shallots, peeled and sliced
1 cup red wine vinegar
2 cups balsamic vinegar
⁵/₈ cup fresh hops *(available from homebrew supply shops)*
¹/₄ cup honey
³/₄ teaspoon kosher salt
1 teaspoon freshly ground black pepper
2 cups olive oil

FOR THE SALAD:
6 cups mixed baby greens
³/₄ cup hops vinaigrette
12 cherry or grape tomatoes
1 cucumber, sliced
1 cup carrots, sliced or shredded
¹/₂ cup blue cheese
4 teaspoons sunflower seeds, shelled

1. Make the vinaigrette: In a deep pot, combine all the ingredients except the oil, and blend with a stick blender or hand blender until well incorporated.
2. Add the oil in a slow, steady stream while mixing to emulsify.
3. Toss the mixed greens with ³/₈ cup of vinaigrette and portion onto plates. Toss the tomatoes, cucumber, and carrots in the remaining ³/₈ cup vinaigrette and portion. Reserve leftover vinaigrette in the refrigerator for future use.
4. Garnish with blue cheese and sunflower seeds. Serve.

STONE BRUSCHETTA BLT SANDWICH

Serves 6 to 8

Perfect Pairing: Stone Oaked Arrogant Bastard Ale

FOR THE BRUSCHETTA MIX:

Yields enough for about 6 to 8 sandwiches

3 cups roma tomatoes, halved, seeded, sliced ¼-inch thick

¼ cup basil, chiffonade (chopped into small, thin strips)

¼ cup red onion, small dice

1 teaspoon garlic, chopped

¼ cup balsamic vinegar

⅛ cup olive/canola oil blend

Kosher salt, to taste

FOR THE ROASTED GARLIC & LEMON MAYONNAISE:

6 egg yolks

⅛ cup fresh lemon juice

1 cup canola oil

1½ teaspoons kosher salt

¼ cup roasted garlic

FOR EACH SANDWICH:

½ cup bruschetta mix

2 tablespoons roasted garlic & lemon mayonnaise

2 tablespoons Carlsbad Gourmet Stone Pale Ale Mustard

Carlsbad Gourmet makes this mustard specially for Stone or you can substitute your favorite whole-grain beer mustard.

1 ciabatta roll, split and toasted

½ cup arugula, washed and dried

3 strips applewood-smoked bacon, cooked

1. Make the bruschetta mix: In a large mixing bowl, combine all the ingredients well. Cover and refrigerate.

2. Make the mayonnaise: Place the egg yolks and lemon juice in a blender. While blender is running, add the oil in thin stream to emulsify. Add salt and roasted garlic until incorporated. Cover and refrigerate.

3. Make the sandwiches: Spread the mayonnaise on the top half of the split roll and spread the mustard on the bottom. Layer the arugula on the bottom, then the bruschetta mix, and top with the bacon. Replace the top of the roll and cut in half diagonally.

4. Serve with your favorite spicy chips.

STONE'S BBQ DUCK TACOS
Serves 8

with Black Beans, Pineapple Salsa, Spanish Rice, and Salsa Fresca

Perfect Pairing: Stone Arrogant Bastard

FOR THE DUCK CONFIT:
Yields 6 cups meat

3 tablespoons kosher salt
4 cloves garlic, smashed
1 shallot, peeled and sliced
8 duck legs with thighs
Freshly ground black pepper, to taste
8 cups duck fat

FOR THE BLACK BEANS:
Yields 6 cups

1 pound black beans, washed
4 cups vegetable stock
1 tablespoon kosher salt
1 tablespoon cayenne pepper

FOR THE SALSA FRESCA:
Yields 4 cups

4 cups tomato, 1/4-inch dice
1/3 cup cilantro, chopped
1/3 cup yellow onion, 1/4-inch dice
1/3 cup jalapeño chile, 1/8-inch dice
1/3 cup lime juice
Kosher salt and freshly ground black
  pepper, to taste

FOR THE PINEAPPLE SALSA:
Yields 2 1/2 cups

2 cups pineapple, peeled and diced (can
  substitute mango or peaches)
1 tablespoon habañero chile, seeded, finely
  chopped (more or less as desired)
1/4 cup red onion, finely chopped
1/8 cup cilantro, chopped
1/8 cup lime juice

FOR THE SPANISH RICE:
Yields 5 cups

Canola/olive oil blend, as needed

1/4 cup onion, chopped
1 clove garlic, chopped
2 cups short grain brown rice
1/2 cup heirloom tomato sauce (use your
  favorite kind or make your own)
3 cups water
1 tablespoon kosher salt
1 tablespoon freshly ground black pepper

FOR THE DUCK TACOS:

2 cups black beans
2 pounds duck confit, pulled and shredded
2 cups salsa fresca
2 cups pineapple salsa
2 cups Spanish rice
1/2 cup Stone Smoked Porter & Pasilla
  Pepper BBQ Sauce
16 small corn tortillas
1 pound Asiago cheese, shredded
2 ounces microgreens

1. Prepare the confit: Sprinkle 1 tablespoon of salt in the bottom of a dish or plastic container large enough to hold the duck pieces in a single layer. Evenly scatter half of the garlic and shallots in the container. Arrange the duck, skin-side up, over the salt mixture, then sprinkle with the remaining salt, garlic, and shallots and the black pepper. Cover and refrigerate for 1 to 2 days.

2. Prepare the black beans: Place the beans in a large bowl, cover with water, and soak overnight. Strain off the water from the beans. In a large pot, simmer beans and vegetable stock over medium heat until the beans are soft. Season with salt and cayenne. Reserve.

3. Make the confit: Preheat the oven to

225°F. Melt the duck fat in a saucepan. Remove the duck from its container, and brush with the salt and seasonings used with the duck. Arrange the duck pieces in a single snug layer in a high-sided baking dish or ovenproof pan. Pour the melted fat over the duck pieces, completely covering the duck with the fat. Place the confit in the oven. Cook for 3 to 4 hours, until the meat pulls easily away from the bones. Remove the pieces from the fat. Be careful, it will be extremely hot. Let the duck cool, then remove the meat from the bones. Discard the bones or save for stock. Heat the shredded duck in the BBQ sauce.

4. Make the salsa fresca: In a large bowl, combine all the ingredients and refrigerate up to 1 day.

5. Make the pineapple salsa: In a large bowl, combine all the ingredients and refrigerate up to 1 day.

6. Make the Spanish rice: In a large saucepan, heat the oil and sauté the onions and garlic until translucent. Remove the onions and garlic from the pan and set aside. Briefly sauté the rice in the same saucepan to brown it slightly. Add the tomato sauce, onions, and garlic. Add water to the rice mixture and bring to a boil. Cover and lower heat to a simmer. Cook 35 minutes until all the liquid is absorbed and the rice is tender. Season with salt and pepper.

7. To serve: Place heated duck on top of each tortilla and garnish with asiago cheese, salsa fresca and microgreens. Serve with the Spanish rice and black beans, then top the beans with the pineapple salsa.

SPICY ALMOND TILAPIA IN HONEY-BUTTER SAUCE   Serves 4

with Toasted Barley and Quinoa Tabouleh and Green Beans with Maitake Mushrooms

Perfect Pairing: Stone Cali Belgique IPA

FOR THE TILAPIA:

4 tilapia fillets
3 tablespoons olive or canola oil, for frying
4 cups toasted barley and quinoa tabouleh
4 (6-ounce) servings green beans and
   maitake mushrooms
¼ cup toasted, sliced almonds, for garnish
Microgreens, for garnish

FOR THE TOASTED BARLEY AND
   QUINOA TABOULEH:

Yields 4 cups

½ cup pearled barley
3½ cups water
1 cup quinoa (rinsed if not prerinsed)
¾ cup fresh lemon juice
¼ cup canola/olive oil blend
1 cup parsley, chopped
1 tablespoon garlic, chopped
1 tablespoon mint, chopped
2 cups tomatoes, seeded, small dice
1 tablespoon red wine vinegar
Kosher salt and freshly ground black
   pepper, to taste

FOR THE TILAPIA CRUST:

1 cup almonds, sliced
1 cup Panko bread crumbs
1 serrano chile, seeded
1 teaspoon red chile flakes
¼ cup all-purpose flour
½ teaspoon kosher salt

FOR THE TILAPIA SAUCE:

Yields 1½ cups

½ cup white wine
¼ cup white wine vinegar

1 teaspoon black peppercorns, crushed
2 teaspoons shallots, chopped
½ bay leaf
½ cup heavy cream
½ pound unsalted butter, cold, cubed
1 tablespoon honey

FOR THE GREEN BEANS AND MAITAKE
   MUSHROOMS:

Yields 4 (6-ounce) servings

2 tablespoons olive/canola oil blend
1 clove garlic, minced
¼ cup leek, sliced thin (optional)
1 pound green beans
½ pound maitake mushrooms, cleaned
   and sliced
Kosher salt

1. Make the tabouleh: In a dry sauce pan, toast the barley over low heat until it is slightly browned and nutty smelling, about 5 minutes. Be careful not to burn it. Add 1½ cups water to the barley and bring to a simmer. Cook approximately 50 minutes until all the water is

absorbed. Remove from stove and let cool. In a separate saucepan, bring the quinoa and 2 cups of water to a simmer. Cook until water is absorbed and the grains are tender (about 15 minutes). Strain off any excess liquid and allow to cool. Once both grains have cooled, mix them together with the remaining ingredients, and season with salt and pepper. Set aside.

2. Make the tilapia crust: Using a food processor, mix together all the ingredients until thoroughly combined.

3. Make the tilapia: Preheat the oven to 400°F. In a medium sauté pan, heat the oil until very hot. Coat the tilapia with the crust mix on all sides and pan sear until crispy (it should only take 1 to 2 minutes per side). Finish cooking in the oven for approximately 5 minutes (depending on thickness of filet).

4. Make the sauce: In a small saucepan, combine the wine, vinegar, peppercorns, shallots, and bay leaf and bring to a simmer. Reduce the liquid until almost dry, then add the cream. Bring back to a simmer and reduce until thick. Whisk in the butter one cube at a time until fully incorporated.

5. Cook the green beans: In a sauté pan, heat the oil to hot. Cook the garlic and leeks briefly, until soft but not yet browned. Add the green beans and mushrooms and sauté until the beans are just tender. Season to taste with salt and pepper.

6. To serve: Spread a generous spoonful of sauce on the plate. Place one scoop of tabouleh and one portion of green beans on the plate, and lay the tilapia over both. Garnish with sliced almonds and microgreens.

BLUE CHEESE JALAPEÑO CHEESECAKE

with Blueberry Compote

Makes 1 (10-inch) cheesecake

Perfect Pairing: Stone Smoked Porter

FOR THE CHEESECAKE:
2 pounds cream cheese
10 ounces granulated sugar
8 eggs
½ cup heavy cream
18 ounces Rogue Smokey blue cheese,
   or similar, grated medium fine
4 ounces jalapeños, hulled and seeded,
   finely diced

FOR THE COMPOTE:
Yields enough for 1 (10-inch) cheesecake
1 pound fresh blueberries
2 ounces jalapeños, hulled and diced
5 ounces granulated sugar

1. Make the cheesecake: In a mixer with a paddle attachment, cream together the cream cheese and the sugar for 10 minutes on low speed.
2. Add eggs and cream, alternating each in three batches.
3. Scrape and mix until smooth.
4. Remove from mixer.
5. Fold in the blue cheese and jalapeños. Pour into a 10-inch springform pan and bake in water bath at 200ºF. for 3 to 4 hours, or until the cake has set fully and has an internal temperature of 170ºF. Remove from oven and cool.
6. Make the blueberry compote: Cook all of the ingredients in a sauce pan over high heat for 5 minutes. Remove from heat and let cool in refrigerator.
7. To serve: Slice cheesecake and generously top with blueberry compote and fresh mint.

WHITE LABS

EVERYONE KNOWS WHAT MALTS AND HOPS CONTRIBUTE TO BEER, but only relatively few beer fans understand the vital role that yeast plays in creating flavors, body, and aromas. The truth is, if you ask an experienced brewer to name the most critical component of flavor creation, he or she will likely say yeast. (There's an old saying: "Brewers make wort, but yeast make beer.")

If you sit down to talk yeast with Chris White — owner and founder of White Labs — you'll understand pretty quickly just how vital yeast is to the brewing process. "Yeast make esters [aroma and flavor compounds] as they grow in the beer," Chris explains. "They consume the sugar and make ethanol and CO_2, but lots of other carbon skeletons are being made at the same time that turn into flavor and aroma compounds. Those leak outside of the yeast cell and get into the finished beer." Chris goes on to explain that there are hundreds of different compounds made by yeast as by-products of fermentation, and each strain makes a different level of those compounds. To illustrate the impact of yeast in brewing, Chris will often do a little experiment for people. "We have the same wort that's been fermented by two different yeasts strains, and people are shocked by the differences," he says. "The strain really changes the profile of a beer."

Chris came to San Diego to attend UCSD in 1991, after receiving his bachelor's degree in biochemistry from UC Davis. While he was working on his PhD dissertation at a yeast lab, he read about an all-grain brewing class being taught by then recent graduate, Yuseff Cherney (now the head brewer at Ballast Point). "We hit it off and wound up brewing all the time together at Yuseff's parents' house in La Jolla," Chris recalls. "At one point, Yuseff and Jack (White) asked me to make yeast for their homebrew store. I thought, well, okay. So, I started White Labs

Below (left to right): Lab Operations Director Neva Parker; yeast strain grows; packaged yeast varieties; testing vials

Chris White has witnessed the explosion of San Diego's beer scene firsthand.

n 1995 to make yeast — originally just for Home Brew Mart." Before he finished school, Chris realized that his yeast hobby could become a full-scale business. When Vince Marsaglia from Pizza Port in Solana Beach asked Chris to make his yeast, White Labs had its first brewery customer. Today, the company banks more than 400 strains, supplies all the San Diego breweries, and sells in 50 other countries.

Since he first arrived in San Diego, Chris has witnessed firsthand the evolution of the city's most talented brewers. "One thing that makes San Diego a little different is that the brewers here started out trying to make some really unique beers," Chris says. "There were very good beers being made in other places, but, for some reason, the brewers here wanted to make even better Belgian style beers, or better hoppy beers, and so they were just thinking out of the box a little bit. When I first started going to conferences, guys like Tomme Arthur (of The Lost Abbey) would go, and Tom Nickel (of O'Brien's Pub) would go, and I can remember when people started noticing them. I think what they were being noticed for was this bent for more creativity. It didn't all work in the beginning — they didn't instantly make what others recognized as great beer. They weren't winning awards at the Great American Beer Festival right away — they were a little bit ahead of their time."

RESOURCES

CRAFT BEER LOVERS' CALENDAR

Belgian Beer Party: During San Diego Belgian Beer Week in July at Pizza Port Carlsbad. The Belgian Beer Party pours some of Belgium's most sought-after beers alongside some of the best Belgian-style offerings in the new world. www.pizzaport.com

Green Flash Anniversary Party: During San Diego Beer Week in November. Green Flash Brewing Co. celebrates its anniversary by inviting plenty of great local breweries to complement its award-winning lineup of beers. Brewmaster Chuck Silva always has some great beers hidden away just for this event. www.greenflashbrew.com

Karl Strauss Beach to Brewery Beer + Music Fest
Every May since 2003, Karl Strauss hosts a beer, beach, and music festival to raise funds for the Surfrider Foundation. In 2011, thousands of fans tasted more than 22 different styles of beer from 60 kegs and hundreds took brewery tours. www.karlstrauss.com

Mission Valley Craft Beer Festival: Every March at The Handlery Hotel (Hotel Circle North). This relatively new event kicks off the beer festival season in San Diego by offering unlimited food and beer from more than 20 local breweries and 20 local chefs. A great lineup of San Diego bands provides music, and all proceeds go to charity. (619) 298-0511

2011 Mission Valley Craft Beer Festival

San Diego Beer Week: Every November. SDBW has become the premier beer event in town with more than 400 events all over the county in 2010. Brewers from as far away as Belgium come to participate during this celebration in America's Craft Beer Capital. www.sdbw.org

San Diego Brewers Guild Festival: During San Diego Beer Week in November at Liberty Station. This festival features every San Diego brewery showing off their best. With nearly 30 breweries pouring almost 100 beers, there is simply too much good beer to imbibe in one afternoon. The festival is the opening weekend of SDBW. www.sandiegobrewersguild.org

San Diego Festival of Beer: Every September, this festival (founded in 1994) takes over the streets of downtown San Diego for a fun-filled evening with more than 6,000 beer lovers enjoying the sounds of live music while sampling from over 70 different breweries. www.sdbeerfest.org ➤

DOGGIE BEER BONES

IT ALL STARTED INNOCENTLY ENOUGH. David Crane was a homebrewer who thought it would be fun to use his spent grain to make dog treats for his friends and family. He developed a special recipe using flour, eggs, peanut butter, and grain and — during the holidays — he would make a few dozen with cookie cutters, wrap them up, and give them as gifts. The treats were such a hit (with dogs and their owners alike), that David soon began making more and more and giving them to a wider range of people. Then he decided to try actually selling them.

"Back in June 2010, I started bagging 'em and tagging 'em," David recalls, "and now I'm up to about 6,000 treats per month." Though he's invested in some equipment that helps make production easier, David is still limited to batches of 90 treats maximum at a time. That means he's doing about 70 full batches per month.

In January 2011, Doggie Beer Bones launched a new product line in cooperation with Stone Brewing Co. — the Stone Bones product line. These doggie treats, which are made from 100% spent grain that went into making Stone beer, were instantly popular with Stone followers as well as other craft beer enthusiasts. David started out producing 50 12-packs per month for Stone, but — within two or three months — he was delivering more than 400 12-packs per month. As David says, "That's 4,800 treats just for them — that's a lot of treats."

Doggie Beer Bones can be found at some San Diego Farmers' Markets, and at various San Diego breweries, and as far away as North Carolina and New York City, where they can be found at "Doggie Island" on City Island in Manhattan.

San Diego International Beer Festival: Three-day festival in June during the San Diego County Fair. The county's biggest beer festival features 400 different beers as well as a competition that draws more than 700 entries from more than 15 countries. www.sdfair.com/beer

San Diego Real Ale Festival: Every spring at Pizza Port Carlsbad. This festival features nothing but cask conditioned ales, all unfiltered and naturally carbonated. Every beer is served through a British beer engine. www.pizzaport.com

San Diego Strong Ale Festival: The weekend after Thanksgiving at Pizza Port Carlsbad. One of San Diego's oldest beer festivals pours nothing under 8% alcohol. www.pizzaport.com

Stone Anniversary Party: August at Cal State University – San Marcos. San Diego's best-known brewery hosts a giant invitational beerfest and fund-raiser for charity every year for its anniversary. In addition to lots of great Stone and other locally brewed beers, there are vintage and import rarities available for sampling, as well as gourmet food options and homebrewed sodas. www.stonebrew.com

Stone Sour Fest: June at Stone Brewing World Bistro & Gardens. Pucker up for hours of sours in celebration of the amazing world of tart and tasty ales! www.stonebrew.com

NATIONAL AND INTERNATIONAL EVENTS

American Craft Beer Week: Known as The Mother of all Beer Weeks, American Craft Beer Week celebrates craft brewers and craft beer culture in the United States every May. It's a national celebration across the United States with events at a brewery near you! In 2010, there were more than 600 events hosted by more than 300 different breweries. www.craftbeer.com

Great American Beer Festival: According to the *Guinness Book of World Records*, there is no other place on earth where a beer aficionado can find more beers on tap. Founded in 1982, the Great American Beer Festival is the American brewing industry's top public tasting opportunity and competition. Over three days, attendees can sample more than 2,200 different beers from more than 450 of the nation's finest breweries. Every September in Colorado. www.greatamericanbeerfestival.com

National Homebrewers Conference and National Homebrew Competition: This American Homebrewers Association conference is a fun, educational gathering designed to enhance homebrewers' brewing skills and knowledge and to increase homebrewing camaraderie. Special seminars and events cater to beer enthusiasts and every level of amateur brewers. Every June. San Diego was host of 2011 event; Seattle to host 2012 conference. www.homebrewersassociation.org and www.ahaconference.org

SAVOR: An American Craft Beer & Food Experience: SAVOR is the main beer- and food-pairing event in the United States every June in Washington, D.C. With 65 of the nation's top independent craft brewers participating, this is where beer enthusiasts and foodies can interact directly with some of the greatest brewers and brewery owners in the world. www.savorcraftbeer.com

World Beer Cup: The Brewers Association developed the World Beer Cup® International Competition in 1996 to celebrate the art and science of brewing by recognizing outstanding achievement. Every two years in the spring, a professional panel of beer judges honors the top three beers in nearly 91 categories with gold, silver, and bronze awards. The World Beer Cup, often referred to as "The Olympics of Beer Competitions," is the most prestigious beer competition in the world. Host city for 2012: San Diego. www.worldbeercup.org

WEST COASTER

THE IDEA CAME TO THEM WHILE TRAVELING IN SPAIN AFTER COLLEGE GRADUATION IN 2009. Mike Shess and Ryan Lamb were trying to figure out what exactly they were going to do with their lives when they returned. Mike recalls the discussion: "We said, 'Alright, we both like beer.' I have a background in media, and Ryan has a background in design. So we cooked up this idea: 'Let's start up a newspaper that covers craft beer.'"

Mike, who grew up in a San Diego newspaper family (his father started *North Park News*), was already very familiar with local beer and knew there was a huge craft beer community. "We decided to research the idea to see if anyone else was doing it, and they weren't," Mike explains. "We spent the rest of our time in Spain developing this." A week after they returned to the States in July 2010, Ryan and Mike were at printers getting quotes, talking to art directors, and getting their paper ready to launch for Beer Week in November.

The *West Coaster* staff is a tight-knit group of local San Diegans that have known each other for years. Art director Brittany is a friend of Mike's since kindergarten, and Austin (in advertising) has known

Mike Shess (left) and Ryan Lamb

Mike and Ryan since high school. Ryan explains that "The Godfather of *West Coaster* is our friend Sam Tierney, who writes our 'Into the Brew' column. He's the one who got us into craft beer. And he showed us that — hey — San Diego is where it's at for the craft beer scene."

With the print version and their companion website, Mike and Ryan want *West Coaster* to be "the authority on craft beer news and events in San Diego" as well as a resource for people who want to know more about craft beer. "A great percentage of the population of San Diegans ... have no idea about craft beer," Mike explains. Ryan adds that they want to be "the place you go to find out about events. There's so much going on. One of our main goals is to be the place you go to find out what's going on tonight." "Basically," Mike adds, "we want to be a resource for this community. We're community builders."

FEATURED BREWERIES

AleSmith Brewing Company
9368 Cabot Drive
San Diego, CA 92126
(858) 549-9888
www.alesmith.com

Ballast Point Brewing Company
10051 Old Grove Road
San Diego, CA 92131
(858) 695-2739
www.ballastpoint.com

Breakwater Brewing Co.
101 N. Coast Highway
Oceanside, CA 92054
(760) 433-6064
www.breakwaterbrewing.com

Coronado Brewing Company
170 Orange Avenue
Coronado, CA 92118
(619) 437-4452
www.coronadobrewing
company.com

Green Flash Brewing Co.
6550 Mira Mesa Boulevard
San Diego, CA 92121
(858) 622-0085
www.greenflashbrew.com

Hess Brewing
7955 Silverton Avenue,
Suite 1201
San Diego, CA 92126
(619) 272-9041
www.hessbrewing.com

Home Brew Mart
5401 Linda Vista Road,
Suite 406
San Diego, CA 92110
(619) 295-2337
www.homebrewmart.com

Iron Fist Brewing Co.
1305 Hot Spring Way,
Suite 101
Vista, CA 92081
(760) 216-6500
www.ironfistbrewing.com

Karl Strauss Brewing Company
Main Brewery
5985 Santa Fe Street
San Diego, CA 92109
(858) 273-2739
www.karlstrauss.com

Lightning Brewery
13200 Kirkham Way
Poway, CA 92064
(858) 513-8070
www.lightningbrewery.com

Manzanita Brewing Co.
9962 Prospect Avenue,
Suite E
Santee, CA 92071
(619) 334-1757
www.manzanitabrewing.com

Mission Brewery
1441 L Street
San Diego, CA 92101
(619) 544-0555
www.missionbrewery.com

Mother Earth Brew Co.
2055 Thibodo Road, Suite H
Vista, CA 92081
(760) 599-4225
www.motherearthbrewco.com

New English Brewing Co.
1795 Hancock Street
San Diego, CA 92110
(619) 857-8023
www.newenglishbrewing.com

Pizza Port Brewing Company
571 Carlsbad Village Drive
Carlsbad, CA 92008
(760) 720-7007
www.pizzaport.com
(Other locations: Ocean
Beach, San Clemente, and
Solana Beach.)

Port Brewing Company/ The Lost Abbey
155 Mata Way, Suite 104
San Marcos, CA 92069
(800) 918-6816
www.lostabbey.com

Rock Bottom Restaurant & Brewery, Gaslamp
401 G Street
San Diego, CA 92101
(619) 231-7000
www.rockbottom.com

Rock Bottom Restaurant & Brewery, La Jolla
8980 Villa La Jolla Drive
La Jolla, CA 92037
(858) 450-9277
www.rockbottom.com

Stone Brewing Co.
1999 Citracado Parkway
Escondido, CA 92029
(760) 471-4999
www.stonebrew.com

TAPHUNTER.COM

Jeff "Flash" and Melani Gordon

THE IDEA FOR TAPHUNTER.COM FIRST CAME TO JEFF "FLASH" GORDON OUT OF SHEER NECESSITY. He was a craft beer fan who wanted to know — sometimes on a daily basis — what beers were on tap at local breweries and bars. Keeping up and gathering that information meant checking a variety of websites, newsletters, and blogs each time, which was cumbersome and quickly became tiresome. So, Jeff came up with a better idea: Create a single site that maintains and updates tap information that can be searched and that can be used to easily connect craft beer lovers with the beers they love. "I started recognizing how much time I was spending visiting different bar websites each day to see if anything special was on tap or to make plans for the evening," Jeff recalls. "Then I realized I could build an application that would centralize all of this information onto one website. Once I started building it and discussing it with Mel [his wife] we quickly realized this would be a helpful tool for lots of other beer fans, not just us."

Today, TapHunter is run by both Jeff and his wife, Melani, who explains, "We have complementary skill sets. I am more sales and marketing, and Jeff is the guy who builds and programs our technology and products." Husband-and-wife teams can be tricky, but Melani adds, "We wouldn't have it any other way. We do everything together." TapHunter users can search the site to find their favorite craft beer, or they can search their favorite locations and see what's flowing. TapHunter also serves as an information hub on upcoming craft beer events, and offers forums and platforms for users and drinkers to provide their ratings, insights, and updates.

Apps for the iPhone and Droid have both recently been made widely available, which means TapHunter.com has become even easier to access — particularly for travelers who want to find good craft beer wherever they roam. Since launching TapHunter.com in San Diego, the Gordons have launched sites for Portland, Seattle, Vancouver, Denver/Boulder, Chicago, San Francisco, Austin, Orange County, and Philadelphia. As far as the future goes, the Gordons say their goal is "to be launched in all markets where craft beer is thriving. We love innovating in an old-school world. That's living the dream to us."

OTHER FEATURED BUSINESSES & GROUPS

BARS, TAVERNS & BREWPUBS

Blind Lady Ale House
3416 Adams Avenue
San Diego, CA 92116
(619) 255-2491
www.blindladyalehouse.com

Downtown Johnny Brown's
1220 3rd Avenue
San Diego, CA 92101
(619) 232-8463
www.downtownjohnnybrowns.com

Hamilton's Tavern
1521 30th Street
San Diego, CA 92102
(619) 238-5460
www.hamiltonstavern.com

Live Wire Bar
2103 El Cajon Boulevard
San Diego, CA 92104
(619) 291-7450
www.livewirebar.com

O'Brien's Pub
4646 Convoy Street
San Diego, CA 92111
(858) 715-1745
www.obrienspub.net

BEER COMMUNITY MEMBERS

Chicks for Beer @ The High Dive
1801 Morena Boulevard
San Diego, CA 92110
(619) 275-0460
www.facebook.com/chicksforbeer
www.highdiveinc.com

Doggie Beer Bones
www.doggiebeerbones.com

PubCakes
7229 El Cajon Boulevard
San Diego, CA 92115
(619) 741-0530
www.pubcakes.com

QUAFF Homebrewers Association
www.quaff.org

TapHunter
www.taphunter.com

West Coaster
www.westcoastersd.com

White Labs
9495 Candida Street
San Diego, CA 92126
(858) 693-3441
www.whitelabs.com

RESTAURANTS

Marine Room
2000 Spindrift Drive
La Jolla, CA 92037
(866) 644-2351
www.marineroom.com

Terra American Bistro
7091 El Cajon Boulevard
San Diego, CA 92115
(619) 293-7088
www.terrasd.com

**The Grill at The Lodge
at Torrey Pines**
11480 North Torrey Pines Road
La Jolla, CA 92037
(858) 453-4420
www.lodgetorreypines.com

URGE Gastropub
16761 Bernardo Center Drive
San Diego, CA 92128
(858) 673-8743
www.urgegastropub.com

OTHER GREAT BREWERIES, BREWPUBS, TAVERNS & BARS

Alpine Beer Company
2351 Alpine Boulevard
Alpine, CA 91901
(619) 445-2337
www.alpinebeerco.com

Back Street Brewery
15 Main Street, Suite 100
Vista, CA 92084
(760) 407-7600
www.lamppostpizza.com

The Beer Company
602 Broadway
San Diego, CA 92101
(619) 398-0707
www.thebeerco.net

The Brewhouse at Eastlake/Bay Bridge Brewing
871 Showroom Place
Chula Vista, CA 91914
(619) 656-2739
www.brewhouseeastlake.com

Callahan's Pub & Brewery
8111 Mira Mesa Boulevard
San Diego, CA 92126
(858) 578-7892
www.callahanspub.com

Churchill's Pub
887 W. San Marcos Boulevard
San Marcos, CA 92078
(760) 471-8773
www.churchillspub.us

Eleven
3519 El Cajon Boulevard
San Diego, CA 92104
(619) 450-4292
www.elevensandiego.com

Gordon Biersch
5010 Mission Center Road
San Diego, CA 92108
(619) 688-1120
www.gordonbiersch.com

La Jolla Brew House
7536 Fay Avenue
La Jolla, CA 92037
(858) 456-6279
www.lajollabrewhouse.com

Main Tap Tavern
518 E. Main Street
El Cajon, CA 92020
(619) 749-6333
www.maintaptavern.com

Neighborhood
777 G Street
San Diego, CA 92101
(619) 446-0002
www.neighborhoodsd.com

Newport Pizza & Ale House
5050 Newport Avenue
Ocean Beach, CA 92107
(619) 224-4540

Oggi's Pizza and Brewing Company
Locations: Carmel Mountain, Del Mar, Eastlake, Encinitas, Mission Valley, Point Loma (Liberty Station), and Santee
www.oggis.com

Pacific Beach Ale House
721 Grand Avenue
San Diego, CA 92109
(858) 581-2337
www.pbalehouse.com

Ritual Tavern
4095 30th Street
San Diego, CA 92104
(619) 283-1618
www.ritualtavern.com

San Diego Brewing Company
10450 Friars Road, Suite L
San Diego, CA 92120
(619) 284-2739
www.sandiegobrewing.com

San Marcos Brewing Company
1080 W. San Marcos Boulevard
San Marcos, CA 92078
(760) 471-0050
www.sanmarcosbrewery.com

SD Tap Room
1269 Garnet Avenue
San Diego, CA 92109
(858) 274-1010
www.sdtaproom.com

Small Bar
4628 Park Boulevard
San Diego, CA 92116
(619) 795-7998
www.smallbarsd.com

Toronado
4026 30th Street
San Diego, CA 92104
(619) 282-0456
www.toronadosd.com

GREAT BOTTLE SHOPS

Bacchus Wine Market
647 G Street
San Diego, CA 92101
(619) 236-0005
www.shopbacchuswine.com

Best Damn Beer Shop
Super JR Market
1036 Seventh Avenue
San Diego, CA 92101
(619) 232-6367
www.bestdamnbeers.com

Beverages 4 Less
9181 Mission Gorge Road
Santee, CA 92071
(619) 448-3773
www.beverages4lessinc.com

Bottle Craft
2161 India Street
San Diego, CA 92101
(619) 487-9493
www.bottlecraftbeer.com

Distiller's Outlet
12329 Poway Road
Poway, CA 92064
(858) 748.4617
www.distillersoutlet.com

Fletcher Hills Bottle Shop
2447 Fletcher Parkway
El Cajon, CA 92020
(619) 469-8410
www.fletcherhillsbottleshop.com

Holiday Wine Cellar
302 West Mission Avenue
Escondido, CA 92025
(760) 745-1200
www.holidaywinecellar.com

KnB Wine Cellars
6380 Del Cerro Boulevard
San Diego, CA 92120
(619) 286-0321
(Plus other Keg N'Bottle locations)
www.knbwinecellars.com

Mesa Liquor & Wine Company
4919 Convoy Street
San Diego, CA 92111
(858) 279-5292
www.sandiegobeerstore.com

Olive Tree Marketplace
4805 Narragansett Avenue
Ocean Beach, CA 92107
(619) 224-0443
www.olivetreemarket.com

Pizza Port Bottle Shop
573 Carlsbad Village Drive
Carlsbad, CA 92013
(760) 720-7007
www.pizzaport.com/locations/
bottle-shop

Royal Liquor
1496 N. Coast Highway 101
Encinitas, CA 92024
(760) 753-4534

Other Places to Check Out:
- Albertsons, www.albertsons.com
- Barons The Marketplace,
  www.baronsmarket.com
- BevMo! stores, www.bevmo.com
- Henry's Markets,
  www.henrysmarkets.com
- Iowa Meat Farms & Siesel's Meats,
  www.iowameatfarms.com
- Major Market,
  www.majormarketgrocery.com
- Piccadilly Marketplace,
  (858) 748-2855
- Ralphs, www.ralphs.com
- Valley Farms Market,
  www.valleyfarmmarkets.com
- Vons, www.vons.com
- Whole Foods, www.wholefoods.com

OTHER BEER RESOURCES

HOME BREW SUPPLIES

American Homebrewing Supply
9295 Chesapeake Drive, Suite E
San Diego, CA 92123
(858) 268-3024
www.americanhomebrewing.com

Home Brews and Gardens
3176 Thorn Street
San Diego, CA 92104
(619) 630-2739
www.homebrewsandgardens.com

Home Brew Mart
5401 Linda Vista Road, Suite 406
San Diego, CA 92110
(619) 295-2337
www.homebrewmart.com

Homebrew 4 Less
9181 Mission Gorge Road
San Diego, CA 92071
(619) 448-3773
www.homebrew4lessinc.com

Hydrobrew
1319 S. Coast Highway
Oceanside, CA 92054
(760) 966-1885
www.hydrobrew.com

Mother Earth Brew Co.
2055 Thibodo Road, Suite H
Vista, CA 92081
(760) 599-4225
www.motherearthbrewco.com

BEER PUBLICATIONS, BLOGS & WEBSITES

- *All About Beer Magazine*
  www.allaboutbeer.com
- Beer Advocate
  www.beeradvocate.com
- Beer Connoisseur
  www.beerconnoisseur.com
- *Beer Magazine*
  www.thebeermag.com
- *Beer West Magazine*
  www.beerwestmag.com
- *Brew: The How-To Homebrew Beer Magazine*
  BYO.com
- *Celebrator*
  www.celebrator.com
- *Draft Magazine*
  www.draftmag.com
- *Imbibe Magazine*
  www.imbibemagazine.com
- PubQuest
  www.pubquest.com
- San Diego Beer Blog
  www.sandiegobeerblog.com
- San Diego Is Brewing Blog
  www.sandiegoisbrewing.com
- *Taps: The Beer Magazine*
  www.tapsmagazine.com
- The Full Pint
  www.thefullpint.com
- *Zymurgy*
  www.homebrewersassociation.org

BEER TOURS

Brewery Tours of San Diego
(619) 961-7999
www.brewerytoursofsandiego.com

Brew Hop San Diego
(858) 361-8457
www.brewhop.com/sandiego

**Five Star Tours &
Charter Bus Company**
(619) 232-5040
www.fivestartours.com

To stay on top of San Diego's ever-changing craft beer scene, check out the *West Coaster's* interactive map: www.westcoastersd.com/directory

INDEX

RECIPE INDEX

BEER INDEX

A Complete Listing of Specific Beers Mentioned in the Text